The
PERSONAL LIBERATION SYSTEM

Inner Freedom
Through the Practice of
Dispassion and Meditation

STEVEN REDDEN

PLS Publications
Ojai, California

Thank you to Deborah, Keera, John, Judy, Melinda, Serena, and Tim for your critiques, suggestions, and proofreading of the text; and to John, Marshall, Michael, Mitzi, Svetlana, and Vienna for your help in designing and creating the cover. Thank you most of all to Robin—without your encouragement and tireless help in all areas, this book would never have become what it is.

Copyright © 2016 by Steven Redden

FIRST EDITION

All rights reserved. No part of this publication may be reproduced, stored in a retrieval system, or transmitted in any form or by any means —electronic, mechanical, photocopying, recording, or otherwise—without written permission in advance from the author, except in brief quotations in critical articles or reviews.

Published by PLS Publications, Ojai, CA
email: info@thepls.org
web site: www.thepls.org

First Printing, 2016
ISBN: 978-0-9646673-1-0
Library of Congress Control Number: 2016938626

Printed by CreateSpace

Permission to use copyrighted material granted courtesy of the Sri Ram Foundation (talks of Baba Hari Dass); Sri Ramanasramam (writings of Ramana Maharshi); the Agni Yoga Society (books on Agni Yoga); and the American Greeting Corporation (greeting card cover).

Cover art derivative of *Blue Water Lily* © Thomas Totz (www.flickr.com/photos/def110/2975222829)
Licensed under Creative Commons "CC BY SA-2.0"
(https://creativecommons.org/licenses/by-sa/2.0/)
Lotus icon by Freepik from www.flaticon.com

CONTENTS

Introduction 5

PART I: THE PRACTICE OF DISPASSION

1   The Basis of Dispassion 11
2   The Necessity for Dispassion 17
3   The Science of Dispassion 26
4   Seeking & Accepting Facts 43
5   Expecting Nothing 56
6   Rejecting Unnecessary Seriousness 67
7   Learning Through Experimentation 76
8   Minding Our Own Business 89
9   Curbing Needless Speculation 108
10 Forgetting the Past 117
11 Controlling Speech 126

PART II: MEDITATION

12 The Basis of Meditation 141
13 The Necessity for Meditation 150
14 Beginning Meditation 156
15 Mind as a Movie Theater 163
16 Mind as a Concept Creator 175

Afterword 189
Bibliography 190

INTRODUCTION

Many years ago I found myself desperate to solve my principal life-problem. From my earliest youth my interior life-experience was one of a pronounced duality. In the background of my consciousness I was aware of an ever-present, unchanging Self or "I" that was independent of my thoughts, feelings, or body. Periodically this wondrous energy that was the real Me would come forward and inhabit my outward persona, so that I *was* It. Temporarily united with this Self, I felt exhilarated, invincible, fearless, ageless, insightful, compassionate, and, above all, *free*—free to be myself, free from the world and its demands, free from the flaws and faults in my lower nature.

The foreground of my awareness consisted of my ordinary human self. As this self, I was afflicted with a painful and distressing predisposition constantly to be thrown into agitation by events, circumstances, and interactions with people. These agitated reactions took every form imaginable: fear, impatience, futility, self-pity, criticism, anger, frustration, irritation, self-doubt, possessiveness, discouragement, humorlessness, and on and on. This problem cast a dispiriting shadow over every aspect of my personal life. Under its oppressive influence, I felt hopelessly in *bondage*—robbed of self-confidence, censored in self-expression, constrained in my relations with others, blocked from being myself.

Not surprisingly, the balance of this duality was decidedly lopsided: the moments of full communion with my real "I" were relatively infrequent and brief, while the tormenting reactions to life were continuous and relentless. Eventually I could no longer stand the misery inflicted by this situation, and I resolved to find a way to free myself from it. What I wanted was simple: to open a pathway to my real and higher "I," so that I could contact it at will and make my experience of it continuous and permanent; and to put an end to all the agitated reactions to people, events, and circumstances that plagued my life and eclipsed the real Me. But how to do it?

After researching various teachings and listening to my intuition and common sense, I was convinced that my two problems were so interrelated that whatever methods I found to address each one separately must work together as a system. Only in this way would they ever generate enough power to accomplish my two goals. As for the "pathway to the Self" problem, it seemed clear that I would solve it through meditation; it was merely a matter of experimenting to find the right kind. The "constant agitated reactions" problem was more of a mystery. In my reading I had run across the word *dispassion*, which had struck a powerful chord in me. I could feel the wonderful and familiar higher calm it represented, and my intuition whispered that here was the solution to the agitation I suffered. Intrigued, I searched through numerous books to discover the science behind it and the step-by-step methods of practicing it. But all I found were sentences like "Through dispassion the Self can dissociate itself from the not-self; this is liberation" and "Dispassion is the Way; through it is one freed." I realized that if I wanted to practice dispassion, I would have to work out the science and create the techniques for it myself.

During my researches I had identified a number of disciplines (also lacking specifics) that I sensed ought to form part of a dispassion practice. So I gathered up all the practical hints about these that I could find and began my quest. After a years-long process of thought, analysis, and experimentation, I succeeded in developing a complete science of dispassion: what it is, why it is necessary, what causes agitated reactions, and how to end them using a collection of specific methods. I then repeated the process for meditation and created a simple, powerful technique that blended seamlessly with the dispassion methods and worked flawlessly for me and others who used it. I now had the integrated program that I envisioned for setting myself free, which I decided to call the Personal Liberation System (PLS). Here is a synopsis of its two components and their relation:

1. The practice of dispassion is based on an understanding of the duality of the higher and lower natures. It consists of adopting a new attitude toward life situations, a new conception of problems, and a new ideal of success; then of applying these three using techniques related to the following topics: facts, expectations, seriousness, experimentation, minding one's own business, speculation, the past, and speech.

2. The meditation is based on an understanding of the duality of Self and not-self, as well as of the structure and operation of the human psychological system. It consists of a basic technique for withdrawing the attention from the outward-turned mind and redirecting it inward to the Self, plus advanced techniques to address the phenomena of inner movies, concepts, and the I-thought.

3. These two components are designed to be used simultaneously and in tandem, as a system. The magic of such a system is that the two do not just combine to make a sum, but multiply each other's beneficial effects: meditating creates a reservoir of calm that makes practicing dispassion easier, and quelling agitated reactions to life makes it easier to meditate.

Since creating the system, I have steadily used it myself, as well as taught it to many others interested in trying its methods. These experiences have enabled me to both refine the techniques and adapt them for general use. When I was satisfied that the PLS was ready for a wider audience and would serve all its users well, I undertook to write this book. My goal was to structure it in such a way that it would serve as both a concise instruction manual and a handy reference source.

Dispassion and meditation are two separate studies, so each is treated in its own section. Dispassion is presented first, for several reasons. It is easier to learn and practice than meditation. It requires no special conditions like silence, solitude, or a time slot in your schedule. And most important, everyone can use it: no matter what sorts of people, situations, and events constitute your particular daily life, they will serve as a rich laboratory for learning and employing the dispassion techniques.

Both the dispassion and meditation sections begin with chapters explaining the basis of, necessity for, and science behind their particular discipline, followed by chapters presenting specific techniques for practicing it. These latter typically follow a fixed format: analyze a problem, explain the technique for solving it, give exercises and experiments for implementing the technique, show how a person might apply the technique to a common life situation, and summarize the chapter's main points for later reference.

As for learning and using the PLS, the following suggestions will lead to the best results. Read the book in order; in the PLS, everything is connected to everything else, so the explanations and techniques presented in one chapter are crucial to those in the next. Use the dispassion and meditation components together to get the full benefit of each. Adopt a scientific attitude that allows you to experiment widely, freely, and imaginatively in the laboratory of your life, so that the techniques can produce their effects. Persevere with the discipline: meditation and the practice of dispassion are cumulative activities that produce results over time.

In the years since its completion, the PLS has been used by people with a variety of motives and goals—treading the spiritual path, discovering their real Self, overcoming troublesome psychological patterns, or simply growing and expanding to be a better person and have a better life. Behind all these strivings is a common theme: all human hearts love freedom, and all human souls yearn for release from limitation and bondage. The Personal Liberation System has proven itself a powerful tool for answering the yearning for inner freedom and self-mastery. It is my hope that its principles and methods will serve you as well as they have served me in this noble quest.

STEVEN REDDEN
September, 2015
Ojai, California

Part I
Dispassion

1

THE BASIS OF DISPASSION

A. The Higher & Lower Natures

Consider the following list of common human qualities:

generosity	kindness	vanity	compassion
cruelty	greed	self-pity	irritation
intolerance	confidence	serenity	love

Most people, if asked to divide the qualities into logical categories of their choosing, and name the categories, would probably produce an arrangement like this:

Desirable/Pleasant/Good		Undesirable/Unpleasant/Bad	
generosity	compassion	cruelty	irritation
kindness	serenity	greed	vanity
confidence	love	intolerance	self-pity

The ease with which everyone naturally and intuitively recognizes these two categories reflects a basic fact of human life: these qualities are all aspects of what we might call our *higher* and *lower* natures. On the following page is an expanded list—by no means complete—of some common qualities of each type.

Everything about dispassion—what it is, why it is desirable, how to practice it, what it accomplishes—derives from the presence and activity in our psyche of these two natures. So let us begin our study by simply noting the basic facts of their operation and how we experience them. (As you read, make sure that you are aware within yourself of the facts being described, since such awareness is essential to using the dispassion techniques to come.)

Higher-Nature Qualities

benevolence	fairness	independence	optimism
brotherhood	fearlessness	intuition	patience
calmness	freedom	joy	selflessness
charity	generosity	kindness	self-confidence
compassion	goodwill	lightness	serenity
confidence	harmlessness	love	sincerity
creativity	honesty	loyalty	sympathy
courage	humor	magnanimity	tolerance
daring	inclusiveness	objectivity	true friendship

Lower-Nature Qualities

anger	discontent	hopelessness	possessiveness
anxiety	discouragement	humorlessness	resentment
arrogance	dishonesty	intolerance	selfishness
conceit	disloyalty	irritation	self-pity
cowardice	envy	jealousy	separateness
critical spirit	fear	laziness	self-deception
cruelty	futility	miserliness	self-doubt
depression	greed	moodiness	vanity
despair	hatred	pessimism	worry

They are energies.

All higher- and lower-nature qualities are names of energies. Like their physical counterparts, these psychic energies exist in two states. Sometimes they are potential energy, temporarily lying dormant as only inclinations or dispositions: "He has a tendency to become irritated and critical." Other times they are kinetic energy, aroused and in motion: "She responded calmly and compassionately to my misfortune."

When in this latter active state, two factors distinguish the way we experience these energies: vibration and weight. The distinctive vibration of the lower nature is best described by the word *agitation*: energies like anger, irritation, worry, and fear vibrate jarringly, often violently, always unpleasantly. The lower nature's distinctive weight is heaviness: depression, despair, futility, and the like make us feel burdened, oppressed, sluggish, sinking.

The higher nature has the opposite characteristics. The vibration of energies like serenity, patience, and tolerance is calm, smooth, harmonious, and always pleasant. The higher nature always feels light in weight: freedom, confidence, and fearlessness, for example, stimulate us to feel unburdened, buoyant, uplifted.

They are connected to specific locations in the body.
We feel the lower-nature vibrations in our solar plexus (gut). When aroused, they often churn and writhe in the pit of our stomach. Simultaneously, our chest can feel narrowed, tight, tense, and our forehead can ache from the commotion their agitation causes in our mind.

We experience the higher-nature vibrations in our heart. When active, they make our whole chest cavity feel expansive, relaxed, open, light. At the same time, the pit of our stomach is calm and unagitated, and we often register insights and intuitions in the center and back part of our head.

They are usually activated by a provocation.
Even though these energies reside within us, they are most often activated and set into motion by our interactions with people and events in the outside world: "I was fired from my job, and I feel angry and humiliated"; "A friend encouraged me, and now I feel confident and optimistic." The same effect is produced when we relive in the present a provocation that occurred in the past: "Thinking back over yesterday's phone call, I felt worried and stressed all over again."

They often arise together.
Commingled as they are in the human psyche, the two natures are frequently activated in tandem and experienced as a package:

> A wealthy businessman feels inspired by compassion and pity to fund a home for battered women and their children. He envisions it nurturing and uplifting them, giving them opportunities to grow and evolve. Simultaneously, he dreams of the home being named after him, and glories in the thought of others publicly recognizing and praising him as an exemplary person.

> A woman registers intuitively that her present relationship is unhealthy and not in her or her partner's best interest. When she imagines ending it, she feels free, joyous, unburdened, and back on the right track. Simultaneously, she feels terrified of being alone, full of self-doubt that she is lovable, and worried that she will be unable to find a place to live and support herself.

This blending and fusing of the two aspects produces the phenomenon we call "human nature"—the state of mixed motive and perpetual tug-of-war between competing energies.

They conflict with each other.

The higher and lower natures are strikingly dissimilar. In fact, many qualities on our earlier list are direct opposites:

tolerance–intolerance	self-confidence–self-doubt
love–hate	optimism–pessimism
patience–impatience	good humor–humorlessness
calm–agitation	honesty–dishonesty
fearlessness–fear	generosity–miserliness

This essential incompatibility of energies trapped in the same container causes conflict, warfare, and stress as they battle each other for expression and control of our psyche.

They both activate the mind, which is neutral.

The mind is equally responsive to both natures, its lines of thought determined by whichever vibration impinges on it. If, for example, we feel irritated in response to something someone says, the mind will replay the words, brood over their inappropriateness or injustice, criticize the speaker's character flaws that caused the speech, and so on. If instead we feel inspired, the mind will produce thoughts of new possibilities and directions, insights into overcoming limitations, creative solutions to problems, and the like.

They can both be activated *by* the mind.

The mind can also initiate lines of thought on its own which in turn provoke the higher or lower energies. Brooding over limitations and past failures, for instance, might stir up self-doubt, futility, and pessimism; whereas the contemplation of volunteering as a reading tutor for underprivileged children might stimulate selflessness, love, and joy.

They affect our mental capabilities.

The activity of the two natures causes variations in our basic mental capacities. Lower-nature energies agitate the mind and hinder concentration. Our thoughts become noisy, disjointed, and irrational. Our mental horizons shrink, and we temporarily lose our sense of perspective and ability to see the big picture. By contrast, higher-nature energies bring calmness, clarity, and focus to the mind. Our thoughts are quiet and rational. We have access to our intuition and our ability to think abstractly.

They determine our character.
The unique blend of higher and lower energies creates a person's character—that collection of habitual tendencies, inclinations, attitudes, and traits that we most often describe as qualities on our list above:

She is kind and generous, usually cheerful, but also vain and quite lazy.

He is confident, courageous, even daring, but impatient with others' mistakes and quick to anger and criticize.

They are our desirable self and undesirable not-self.
We naturally associate the higher-nature qualities with our authentic, best self and our best feelings, and would like to have more of them. Just as naturally, we regard the lower-nature qualities as not really native parts of our true identity, but rather as painful, unwelcome visitors that we would love to be rid of.

B. Summary

Practicing dispassion requires recognizing various energies and being aware of when and how they are manifesting. The list of qualities and the basic facts about the operation of the higher and lower natures that we have considered should serve as a touchstone for that purpose. Specifically,

- When we consider or encounter various human qualities, we will recognize them as energies.
- When our solar plexus churns, we will recognize the activity of our lower nature; when our heart glows, our higher nature.
- When we interact with people and situations, we will recognize when and how they provoke the energies within us.
- When we feel conflicted or torn between two opposite motives, we will recognize the simultaneous operation of both natures.
- When we observe our mind incited to a line of thought, we will recognize one of the two energies as its motivator and director.
- When we freely initiate a line of thought, we will recognize when it is joined by one energy or the other, or both.

- When we are thinking, we will recognize that our mental faculties and capacity vary according to which of the two are active.
- When we consider our own or another's character, we will recognize it as a unique mix of qualified energies.
- When we contrast our central self with the peripheral not-self, we will recognize the two natures as the constituents of those two poles.

2

THE NECESSITY FOR DISPASSION

A. The Case for Practicing Dispassion

Most readers no doubt have an intuitive understanding of the words *agitation* and *dispassion* as we have used them so far. But before proceeding further, let us define these two terms clearly, as they are crucial to both our current appraisal and all the ideas that follow:

- *Agitation:* any vibration motivated or created by the lower nature.
- *Dispassion:* the state of not being thrown into agitation by any person, circumstance, or event.

With these definitions in mind, let us consider the argument against agitation and for dispassion.

The Lower Nature is Painful and Not Fun.

The most compelling reason for practicing dispassion is also the most screamingly obvious: lower-nature energies are painful; they feel bad; they hurt! It is painful to feel energies like despair or anxiety or futility or self-doubt agitating our psyche. No one, during such moments, ever answers "Yes" to the question, "Are we having fun yet?"

Though it is an easy fact to forget when we are agitated, the higher-nature energies feel the opposite: pleasurable, uplifting, fun. When we feel fearless, sympathetic, loving, and free, our suffering vanishes and it is a joy to be alive. Remembering this fact, who would not rather feel generous than miserly, patient than impatient, tolerant than intolerant, calm than agitated?

The Lower Nature Blocks the Higher.

Many higher-nature qualities, as we just noted, have an opposite, "evil twin," lower-nature quality. As long as the lower twin is present and habitually active, it blocks the higher one from expression. Whenever we weaken or remove a particular lower-nature quality—the goal of dispassion—we make room for the appearance of this opposite higher-nature quality, which flows naturally into the vacuum we have created. Thus, removing impatience makes room for patience, hate for love, intolerance for tolerance, agitation for calm, and so on.

The Lower Nature Harms our Physical Body.

Many common lower-nature qualities produce physical stress, long known to be harmful to physical health. Stress is linked to headaches, upset stomach, elevated blood pressure, chest pain, inflammation, and sleep problems; it can also bring on or worsen certain symptoms or diseases. But even without scientific evidence, most people already sense the destructive power of the lower-nature passions: they can feel that when anger, anxiety, fear, hatred, irritation, resentment, and the like are roiling within them, it is not doing anything good to their body.

The higher-nature qualities, along with meditation, have the documented opposite effect: they calm the nervous system, lower blood pressure, reduce stress, and increase immunity, among many other beneficial effects.

The Lower Nature Harms our "Emotional Body."

Perhaps the most serious harm the lower energy can cause occurs in the emotional nature, through what we might call the "habit legacy." We all experience this phenomenon in our physical body. We habituate our stomach to eating at certain times, and it automatically starts growling at those times; we establish a regular bedtime, and we get sleepy at that time. These habits can also be cravings and addictions—to sugar, tobacco, alcohol, painkillers, sleeping pills, etc. Once set, such habits are tenacious and difficult to alter, as we discover when, for example, we travel to a distant time zone or start a new diet or try to quit smoking.

This same phenomenon occurs in our "emotional body." Every lower-nature energy that we permit to agitate it—irritation, criticism, anxiety, humorlessness—simultaneously trains it to vibrate accordingly. When the agitation eventually ends, a vibratory legacy remains: like a robot, our emotional nature has been programmed, and remembers. If the programming is irritation, we now find it a little easier to become irritated; if anxiety, a little easier to become anxious. In this way we create tendencies which, if repeated enough times, become habits. We then find ourselves constantly assaulted by emotions that seem to have a life of their own, arising automatically and uncontrollably when provoked by various people or situations—or perhaps without any provocation at all. Thus, inadvertently and by our own hand, we build a prison of lower-nature habits and character flaws that are difficult to remove.

The same principle of course applies to higher-nature energies. When we contact such energies through meditation, and remove the obstacles to their expression through dispassion, then by the same process we can build their vibrations into our emotional nature and their qualities into our character.

The Lower Nature Harms our Mind.

Higher-nature ideas, intuitions, insights, understanding—what we might call the mental component of the higher nature—are not generated by the mind like ordinary thoughts. Rather, they exist in their own high realm and merely use the mind as a vehicle, so to say, by which to enter our awareness. For this to happen, our mind, or at least a significant part of it, must be quiet and motionless and function as a "receiving plate" on which these higher thoughts register. This idea is beautifully captured in the following passage:

> It is upon the serene and placid surface of the unruffled mind that the visions gathered from the invisible world find a representation in the visible one. —*The Mahatma Letters*, 64.

Naturally, when agitation from the lower nature seizes the mind and spreads throughout it, no "serene and placid surface" exists, and the higher mental gifts temporarily vanish, as if non-existent. This misfortune cuts us off from our Self and its guiding ideas, and our mind reverts to its lower function of "thought-making machine." In this mode, our ability to concentrate often disappears as our attention becomes preoccupied with, or yanked wildly about by, the turbulence from below. Our thoughts become by turns uninspired, pessimistic, disjointed, irrational, discouraged, convinced of unreal limitations. A feedback loop then forms between the mind and the lower emotions, each inflaming the other in a downward spiral.

By contrast, when we retain our mental receptivity to the higher nature, our mind is clear and calm; we concentrate effortlessly; our thoughts are enthusiastic, optimistic, creative, rational, and insightful. An opposite feedback loop forms between the mind and the higher-nature feelings, each inspiring the other in an upward spiral. In either case, when the episode of mental activity ceases, another habit legacy remains: we have accustomed our mind to certain types of vibrations, and it learns to reproduce them easily and readily. Tendencies are thus born which, repeated often enough, become thought-habits—for good or ill—that are powerfully resistant to change.

The Lower Nature Harms Others.

When people smoke, their lit cigarettes and exhalations fill the surrounding air with toxic chemicals. All those nearby are then forced to breathe this second-hand smoke, to the detriment of their health. An analogous situation exists in the subtle energy world. When aroused, not only do lower-nature energies vibrate within us, but they radiate outward, either inflicting themselves directly on others or creating a toxic atmosphere that others must "breathe."

These harmful emanations take numerous forms and produce various effects. Radiations of energies like depression, pessimism, futility, and despair fill the surrounding space with a dark cloud of misery and gloom. Some people's radiations of moodiness, neediness, criticism, resentment, and the like are so pronounced that others feel as if they must constantly "walk on eggshells" in their presence, and regard them as "high maintenance." Other people's radiations turn them into energy vampires, leaving everyone in their wake drained and fatigued. Still others' overbearing and bullying energy infringes the free will of their targets and creates an atmosphere of fear and intimidation. There is virtually no end of different examples we could cite of such "negative energy" and "bad vibes," but in every case their psychic weight drags others down and make their lives harder and unhappier. In addition, all these radiations and atmospheres, like germs, are contagious: they infect the collective consciousness as they spread throughout groups of people, from offices to schools to cities to entire countries.

People who radiate higher-nature energy naturally create an atmosphere with the opposite effects. Some may radiate cheerfulness, optimism, vivacity, and joy, stimulating and uplifting everyone around. We always look forward to being with people with such radiations, and always feel better once we are. Others' higher-nature radiations create an atmosphere of what we might call "warm neutrality." In their presence we sense that we are welcome to be ourselves without being judged or criticized, and that our conflicts and mistakes and shortcomings will be met with sympathy, tolerance, understanding, and humor—a great relief. Still others' radiations of fearlessness, daring, courage, and independence inspire us to experiment, take risks, and step beyond our self-imposed limits. In every case, such people perform a significant service to others through the aura that their particular higher radiations create. They make others' lives better, help to purify the world's thought-atmosphere, and make higher energy available to those receptive to it.

The Lower Nature Harms a Meditation Practice.

[The issues in this final section will be familiar to readers with meditation experience, but perhaps unfamiliar to those without it. The meditation chapters in Part II of this book will address all these ideas in detail.]

Meditating successfully introduces higher-nature energy and qualities into the psyche, where they accumulate as if in a reservoir. Once there, it is essential to guard and retain them, for only then can they gradually infuse themselves into our thoughts and feelings and body to become a permanent part of us. But the moment we stop meditating and turn our attention outward, the lower nature reasserts itself in the form of habitual thoughts, feelings, and reactions. If we have no practice of dispassion by which to resist the pressure of this lower energy, we leave ourselves open to being overrun by it and thrown into agitation of one kind or another. If this happens, our reservoir of higher energy gained from meditation drains quickly away, leaving us with a net gain of zero. It is like running a heater and generating a roomful of warming air, but then opening the windows and letting it all escape.

This squandering of higher energy through a lack of dispassion is bad enough, but the damage does not end there. When it is time to meditate again, we must always first transition from outward mental busyness to inward mental quiet. If our psyche is in an uproar from unregulated and unchecked lower-nature agitation, we have to waste valuable meditation time calming the emotions and stilling the mind before we can even begin. This means less time bathing in the higher energy and thus less "storage" of it, which in turn makes us more susceptible than before to lower-nature provocations. Incidentally, when we are well-stocked with higher energy, the opposite happens: the higher acts as a shield protecting against the lower and making us less susceptible to its incitements. Thus a familiar phenomenon in the outer material world is replicated in the inner energy one: the rich get richer, the poor get poorer.

Conclusion

It should be abundantly clear that lower-nature energies harm ourselves and others in manifold ways, and that we therefore have a compelling interest in subtracting them from our psyche. This is precisely what the PLS is designed to do through its method of dispassion, which we will begin studying in detail in Chapter 3. The opposite is of course true about higher-nature energies: we have an equally powerful interest in adding them to our psyche, using the PLS meditation taught in Part II.

Where dispassion is concerned, a keen awareness of our higher interest is the crucial factor that sets the practice into motion. To activate this awareness, the PLS advises that prior to any act—mental, emotional, or physical—we ask ourselves the "interest question":

Is this action in my higher interest?

Here are some common examples:

- Is it in my higher interest to feel irritated about my boss's decision?
- Is it in my higher interest to join others in criticizing this person?
- Is it in my higher interest to wallow in self-pity?
- Is it in my higher interest to resent my competitor's success?

Once we remember that the answer is "no," and why (see the seven reason listed earlier in this section), our job is then to intervene and govern the lower nature through the dispassion techniques we are soon to learn. *Thus the practice of dispassion is in essence a vigorous energy management program.* In this way it is the same as managing an overhaul of our diet: stop indulging harmful energies/foods, start governing the energies/food we allow into our system, and base all choices on our higher psychological/physical interests. As we study the science of dispassion in the coming chapters, we will repeatedly return to this question of our higher interest, integrating it into each specific technique so that it will soon become second nature to ask it.

B. Dispassion Fears & Misconceptions

Some people initially regard the idea of practicing dispassion with wariness and suspicion, concerned about negative effects that it might produce. Specifically, they fear the following:

- Won't dispassion make me insensitive and unfeeling?
- Won't dispassion make me passive and acquiescent in an unhealthy way?
- Won't dispassion take away my drive and commitment to causes?

Despite their different themes, all these questions have a common origin: confusion about the meaning of the word *dispassion* itself. This confusion is ultimately traceable to dictionary definitions which indiscriminately lump together higher- and lower-nature emotions. Here is a typical example:

- *Passion:* any powerful emotion or appetite, such as love, joy, hatred, anger, or greed.
- *Dispassion*: freedom from passion, bias, or emotion; objectivity.

Anyone reading this naturally forms the erroneous idea that dispassion involves eliminating *all* emotion, higher and lower, thus leaving those who practice it cold, unfeeling, aloof, insensitive, disengaged. But if we rewrite the definitions properly to account for the higher and lower natures—as our earlier definition already does—this misconception vanishes:

- *Passion:* any powerful *lower* emotion or appetite, such as hatred, anger, or greed.
- *Dispassion*: freedom from *lower-nature* passions, bias, or emotions; objectivity.

This simple change clarifies what dispassion truly is—a way to free oneself from undesirable lower emotions *while retaining and expanding all the desirable higher ones*. Understanding this elementary distinction paves the way to satisfactory answers to the three questions so often asked.

1. Won't dispassion make me insensitive and unfeeling?

Actually, it is precisely when we are agitated that we are insensitive and unfeeling. Imagine a pool of water. When its surface is still and calm, it registers and perfectly reflects images in it. When even a light wind ripples the surface, the images immediately become distorted. When the water is positively churning, not only do the images vanish, but all the sediment from the bottom of the pool is stirred up in the water, which is no longer even clear.

An analogous situation exists in our watery emotional nature. Only when dispassion renders it tranquil and undisturbed is its full receptivity available and uncompromised. It is then that we can register our best higher-nature feelings—"soul emotions," if you like—and perceive all the subtle nuances in our interactions with people and circumstances.

But let agitation muddy our emotional waters, and all our best feelings and sensitivity vanish. Our perception and receptivity shrink and become limited to a narrow band of self-centered, lower-nature vibrations, and all our attention focuses on our self—the lower one, not the higher. At such times, it is impossible to really hear a Beethoven symphony or enjoy a beautiful sunset or sympathize with a friend's troubles, because the commotion in our gut and head renders us thoroughly unfeeling and insensitive. Ironically, of course, "unfeeling and insensitive" is the very thing that people fear practicing dispassion will make them!

2. Won't dispassion make me passive and acquiescent in a bad way?

Actually, it is lower-nature qualities like fear, depression, futility, laziness, and pessimism that cause the wrong kind of passivity and acquiescence. By eliminating such qualities, dispassion opens the door to our higher nature, which, though still and quiet, is *dynamic*. This frees us to assert ourselves and act decisively when it is appropriate to do so, and increases our power to effect needed changes.

We might note too that lower-nature energy also causes the opposite of passivity and acquiescence—the wrong kind of reactivity and resistance. Dispassion also eliminates these, freeing us to calmly accept facts and refrain from acting when doing so is appropriate. Thus dispassion restores the proper balance between these pairs of opposites, enabling us to respond to each situation in the way that is most favorable to our own and others' higher interest. (The chapters that follow address these issues in detail.)

3. Won't dispassion take away my drive and commitment to causes?

Actually, the higher nature is the source of the visions and ideals behind all good and noble causes, so becoming more dispassionate will not reduce your commitment and drive; if anything, it will strengthen and increase it. What dispassion *will* do is reduce and eventually remove all the lower-nature agitations that are commingled with that higher inspiration and interfere with its expression. For example, suppose you are a passionate environmental activist whose zeal and drive are mixed with constant anger, frustration, and resentment over environmental destruction, and who has turbulent reactions to every instance of corporate law-breaking, political roadblock, lying propaganda, public complacency, etc. that you encounter about it. Not only are none of these lower agitations necessary to your commitment and drive, they are a positive hindrance to acting effectively on them. Practicing dispassion calms all this pointless agitation, enabling you to think clearly and creatively about how best to affect governmental policy, educate the public, debate opponents, counteract propaganda, use the media, and do anything else necessary to accomplish your goals. It also frees up all the energy formerly consumed by the lower agitation, allowing you to redirect it to vigorous and sustained practical action. Finally, it frees you to be serene and joyful as you work, instead of agitated and frazzled.

C. Summary

- Agitation is any vibration motivated or created by the lower nature.
- Dispassion is the state of not being thrown into agitation.
- Lower-nature energies are painful and not fun.
- Lower-nature energies block corresponding higher-nature ones.
- Lower-nature energies harm our minds, emotional natures, and bodies.
- Lower-nature energies harm other people.
- Lower-nature energies interfere with meditation.
- Subtracting lower-nature energies is vital to our higher interest.
- "Is this action—mental, emotional, physical—in my higher interest?"
- The PLS method of subtracting the lower nature is dispassion.
- Practicing dispassion is a form of energy management.
- "Stop indulging; start governing; become an energy manager."
- Dispassion will not make you insensitive or unfeeling.
- Dispassion will not rob you of idealism and commitment to causes.
- Dispassion will not make you passive or prevent decisive action.

3

THE SCIENCE OF DISPASSION

A. Two Opposite Views of the Cause of "Problems"

A musical analogy

Imagine a room containing two harps, both in tune. If someone plucks a string, say middle C, on Harp #1, its vibrations spread throughout the room, eventually striking against the middle C string on Harp #2, which then also begins to sound. (Acoustics calls this phenomenon "sympathetic resonance.") Now further imagine that we regard middle C as an undesirable tone, and we want to prevent it from ever sounding again on Harp #2, which we own. In the process of considering how best to accomplish this, we realize that two viewpoints are possible about the cause of this problematic vibration in our harp:

1. It is caused by the vibration in Harp #1—if its middle C string had not vibrated, neither would ours.
2. It is caused by our harp's *having a middle C string*—if it had none, the vibration from Harp #1 would produce no effect on it.

Since our ultimate goal is to render our harp permanently immune to sounding middle C, we quickly realize that the second viewpoint ("the cause lies within our own harp") leads to the only surefire, untrumpable method of accomplishing this: remove our C string. If we take this simple action, we solve the problem in one fell swoop, and no amount or type of outer vibratory "provocation" will result in our harp sounding middle C.

Note that if we tried instead the method suggested by the first viewpoint ("the cause lies outside our own harp, in Harp #1"), we might naturally begin by removing Harp #1 from the room, or even destroying it, so that it could no longer "cause" our middle C string to vibrate. That would solve the problem for the present, but we would soon realize that it is not a permanent solution. For what is to stop someone from moving another harp into the room? Or bringing in a clarinet or violin or other instrument that could play middle C? Or singing middle C? Or plucking the middle C in our harp with her finger? The possibilities are infinite and unmanageable: trying to remove every possible external source of a middle C vibration is futile. And even if we could do this, the complexity of trying to exert such control over the ever-changing environment would be a full-time job, leaving us no time to live! So if we insist on complete immunity from this tone, our better choice—and conveniently also the simpler one—is to remove the middle C string from our harp.

The human correspondence

Our emotional nature is an inner replica of a physical harp: each higher- and lower-nature quality is represented by its own individual string, and each string vibrates with its particular "feeling-tone" when activated. Thus we have lower-nature "irritation strings," "fear strings," "vanity strings," as well as higher-nature "compassion strings," "joy strings," "tolerance strings," etc.

Now let us conduct the same analysis that we did above. Imagine that we are in a room with another person, whom we will call Bob. Bob thinks, speaks, or acts, and his resulting "vibration" radiates outward and strikes up against one of our "strings," which begins to "vibrate"—in other words, we have a reaction. Now further imagine that this reaction consists of painful and harmful lower-nature agitation, and that we want to prevent it from ever occurring again. In analyzing how best to achieve this, we realize that two points of view are possible about the cause of our reaction:

1. It is caused by Bob's thought, word, or deed—if he had not acted, we would not have reacted.
2. It is caused by *a lower vibrational tendency in ourselves*—if we did not possess this lower character quality, Bob's actions would produce no effect on us.

Since our ultimate goal is to end this particular lower-nature agitation, we quickly realize, as we did in our musical example, that the second viewpoint ("the cause lies within ourselves") leads to the only permanent method of accomplishing this: remove our lower vibrational tendency or habit. This is, of course, a more difficult task than removing a string from a physical harp with a few turns of a wrench. Yet it can be done using the dispassion (and meditation) techniques explained in the following chapters, so that eventually no amount or type of outer vibratory "provocation" will result in our "inner harp" sounding painful lower-nature agitation.

If instead we try to use the method suggested by the first viewpoint ("the cause lies outside ourselves"), we run into the same insurmountable problem as with the harp: we may escape from or avoid Bob, but someone else will inevitably appear who will provoke the same undesirable agitation in us. And after that person (or circumstance or event) vanishes, another will appear; and then another, and another, without end. In a world with seven billion people and an infinity of possible situations and events, there is simply no escape. Even if the entire outside world vanished, we would still be saddled with vivid memories of it that would possess the same provocative effect. So if we really want to gain permanent immunity from being thrown into agitation, our only realistic option—and the one clearly in our higher interest—is to devote all our resources to removing our own lower-nature "strings." As Samuel Johnson wrote,

> He who has so little knowledge of human nature as to seek happiness by changing anything but his own disposition will waste his life away in fruitless efforts.

B. The Transition to the New View of Problems

Once we decide to cast our lot with the "permanent immunity" option, we must make a major readjustment in our thinking:

- *Discard the old view*: Problems are caused by people, events, and circumstances outside us.
- *Adopt the new view*: Problems are caused by lower-nature energies in our psyche.

In theory, making this transition would appear to be a simple matter, but in practice, many find that the old view is so deeply ingrained and habitual that it is hard to break free from. Yet we must do so before we can successfully use the dispassion techniques to come, since all of them have the new view of problems as their basis and starting point. Therefore, let us identify and dissect the most common obstacles involved, and consider why and how to adjust our concepts. We will begin with a table of examples from daily life that depicts the old view, then analyze it column by column:

The Old View of Problems

Problem	Reaction	Cause
Have a flat tire	Angry, afraid	Tire
Son makes an F in math	Embarrassed, mad	Son, F
Flight is canceled	Furious, stressed	Airline
Lied to by friend	Betrayed, let down	Friend
Rains on day of our picnic	Bitter, self-pitying	Rain
Fired from job	Humiliated, scared	Boss
Driving & hit every red light	Irritated, impatient	Red light
Guilt-tripped by mother	Guilty, resentful	Mother

Column 1: Problem

In the physical world, we experience a wide variety of obvious cause-and-effect sequences. If we are driving a nail with a hammer and hit our finger, the result is pain. If we breathe air loaded with germs, the result is often a cold or the flu or some other contagious illness. In both these cases, and countless others, an outer provocation (hammer, germs) clearly causes an inner reaction or condition (finger pain, illness). So when we experience, say, another person's words, followed instantly by mental and emotional agitation within ourselves, it *feels* identical to the familiar physical cause-effect sequences to which we are so accustomed. Thus, automatically and without really thinking, we designate the former as the cause of the latter, as if the two cases were identical:

Hammer hits finger => physical pain => caused by hammer.
Words hit psyche => emotional pain => caused by speaker.

Interpretations like these in turn lead us to define "problem" as something like "an undesirable event, circumstance, or action that we are unfortunately involved in or made a part of."

The trouble with such interpretations is that they are based on a false analogy between the physical and psychological realms. In the former, a hammer does generate a force that transfers into our finger and produces physical pain, so there our cause-and-effect reasoning is accurate. But in the latter, no force whatsoever emanates from, say, the flatness of a tire, magically passes into our psyche, seizes our emotional nature, and "makes" us angry. Nor does any force emanate from a light turning red that makes us irritated; or from an F on a piece of paper that makes us embarrassed or frustrated; or from rain that makes us bitter. Forces of such kind do not exist; if we imagine that they do, and "reason" that they cause any of our emotions or thoughts, we are tripping.

Now it is true that the thoughts and words that people may direct at us are real (psychic) forces, and not imaginary. But it is also true that such forces—lies from a friend, criticism from a boss, etc.—cannot and do not actually pass into our psyche, take control of it against our will, and "make" us feel or think anything—even though it may feel that way to us before we have thought about it carefully.

Once we really grasp this fact that outer factors possess no inherent problems which they are "raying" at us or somehow transferring into us, our old definition of "problem" becomes untenable. External elements may indeed provoke our problems, but *they are not the problem itself*—just as a messenger is not the contents of the message he delivers. So "Problem" is clearly the wrong heading for Column 1; "Situation" would be a more accurate choice to describe the entries in this column, which are simply the circumstances, events, and people that constitute our outer environment.

Column 2: Reactions

As long as we think of problems as external entities that impose themselves on us, it is natural to believe that they cause reactions which we have no control over or responsibility for—like a finger reacting to a hammer blow. In this conception, we are innocently walking around minding our own business when some situation inflicts itself on us—usually unfairly and undeservingly, as we view it—and transfers a problem into us, "making" us involuntarily feel some particular lower agitation or another. Hence the familiar assertions we hear from others and in our own head: Judy made me angry, Matt hurt my feelings, Kevin's attitude irritated me, the airlines ruined my day, my boss humiliated me, etc.

As we now see, this whole conception does not match the facts: (1) the situations that we supposed were causing our reactions are in truth neutral, have no inherent power, and inflict nothing whatever on us; and (2) we have psyches loaded with lower-nature inclinations, tendencies, and habits of which we are the owners and which often flare up (react) when we encounter various outer situations. And it is precisely these reactions—the agitation produced by our own lower nature—that alone constitute our problem. So, for example, when we feel irritated, the problem we have is the irritation itself, not the person whose words or deeds provoked it. When we feel afraid, the problem we have is the fear itself, not the thing we are afraid of. When we feel sorry for ourselves, the problem we have is the self-pity itself, not some unfair situation or treatment by which we feel victimized. Whatever our lower-nature agitation is, so long as it continues, we have a problem; the moment it stops, our problem ceases to be. Its arising and cessation take place wholly within the confines of our own psyche. Even though it may be provoked by something outside, the agitation is its own thing and is ultimately not about anything other than itself.

Once we digest these facts, it becomes clear that "Problem" is the word that belongs at the head of Column 2. It is not that "Reaction" is wrong; all the entries in the column are in fact lower-nature reactions. But labeling them as "Problem" removes our attention from outer situations and provocations, and focuses it instead within our psyche, where all dispassion techniques must be applied and all reaction-problems solved.

Column 3: Cause

If we were taken hostage, or trapped in an elevator or burning building, we would naturally focus all our attention and energy on how to escape: How can we make a 911 call? How can we untie our hands and get out of the trunk of this car? How do we pry open these elevator doors or get out of this building? For escape purposes, all other types of questions would be irrelevant. For example, we might naturally want to know who or what was responsible for—"caused"—our situation, what their motive was, why it should have happened to us, etc. But we would also know that considering questions like these would not only not help us escape, but actually delay or even prevent it.

This same principle applies to freeing ourselves in the psychological realm. The PLS subscribes to Buddha's idea that concerning liberation, only two questions matter: How am I in bondage? How do I get out of it? (Or, said another way, What is my problem? How do I solve it?) If we have successfully adopted the new view of problems, we would answer thus:

- How am I in bondage? ... I am plagued by a lower-nature agitation.
- How do I get out of it? ... I apply a particular dispassion technique.

Having accurately located our problem within and identified the method for solving it, we would realize that what provoked the agitation —"caused" it, in the old view—is irrelevant. After all, whether it was Joe or Jane or a flat tire or a canceled flight that triggered, say, irritation, the facts are that (1) we are equally irritated either way, (2) irritation is a lower-nature agitation that it is in our higher interest to remove, and (3) the removal process does not involve or require any consideration of what provoked it. Moreover, every moment spent thinking about, resenting, blaming, condemning, fearing, criticizing, etc., the provoking agent of a problem, is a moment not spent applying the dispassion method that will eliminate the problem itself. And even worse, if our attention gets hijacked into endless brooding and fuming over the provocation—what Joe or Jane did, why they did it, how rude or unfair or cruel or stupid it was, how they do this all this time and get away with it, what we would like to see happen to them as punishment, etc.— when we are finished, not only will we still be irritated, but we will have made it worse, and thus harder to remove!

So, given these facts, we really do not even need a Column 3 labeled "Cause." Yet it might be useful to keep it and replace the old entries with "Irrelevant," as a reminder of the attitude we must resolutely cultivate toward them to free our minds to apply the dispassion techniques.

We now have three new column headings for our table to reflect our transition to the new viewpoint:

- *Situation*: an assortment of material conditions, either static or dynamic, arranged in a certain way; an external state of affairs.
- *Problem*: Internal agitation of lower-nature energies in a psyche.
- *Cause of Agitation*: Irrelevant to how we eliminate it.

Inserting these headings produces the revised table on the facing page:

The New, Adjusted View of Problems

Situation	Problem	Cause
Have a flat tire	Angry, afraid	~~Tire~~ Irrelevant
Son makes an F in math	Embarrassed, mad	~~Son, F~~ Irrelevant
Unfair criticism from teacher	Insulted, hurt	~~Teacher~~ Irrelevant
Flight is canceled	Furious, stressed	~~Airlines~~ Irrelevant
Lied to by friend	Betrayed, let down	~~Friend~~ Irrelevant
Rains on day of our picnic	Bitter, self-pity	~~Rain~~ Irrelevant
Fired from our job	Humiliated, scared	~~Boss~~ Irrelevant
Driving & hit every red light	Irritated, impatient	~~Red light~~ Irrelevant
Guilt-tripped by mother	Guilty, resentful	~~Mother~~ Irrelevant

C. A New View of Situations

Unfortunately, acquiring a new interior viewpoint does not magically exempt us from dealing with all the trying exterior situations that life brings us. We still have to address them, contend with them, and often take vigorous, decisive action to change them. What is different, however, is that our new view of problems now leaves us untethered to the agitation we previously imagined was inherent in them. Before, every troublesome situation automatically "forced" us to become agitated. Now, we realize we have a choice: in every situation, we can either (1) have the situation or (2) have the situation, plus add a problem to it by being thrown into agitation about it. If we choose (2), we now have two "problems," the second of which is entirely created by us. The table on the following page shows our choices when applied to previous examples.

Naturally, the practice of dispassion, as well as plain common sense, argues for never again picking Choice #2, for two compelling reasons. First, if we ask ourselves the fundamental PLS question of whether it is in our higher interest to be thrown into agitation about a given situation, and then recall all the effects of such agitation that we catalogued in Chapter 2—painful, not fun; blocks higher nature; harms body, emotions, mind, other people, and meditation—we will answer, "No."

Sample Choices

Choice #1—Situation	Choice #2—Situation + Problem
Have a flat tire	Have a flat tire, plus feel angry
Make a lunch date with a friend who never arrives	Make a lunch date with a friend who never arrives, plus feel hurt
Fired from job	Fired from job, plus feel humiliated
Late driving to work and hit every red light	Late driving to work and hit every red light, plus feel irritated
Son makes an "F" in math	Son makes an "F" in math, plus feel frustrated, embarrassed, let down
Flight is canceled	Flight is canceled, plus feel furious
Rains on the day of picnic	Rains on the day of picnic, plus feel bitter about always having bad luck
Guilt-tripped by mother	Guilt-tripped by mother, plus feel guilty and resentful

There is simply no situation or circumstance, however extreme or unexpected or outrageous or difficult, in which it is in our higher interest to become agitated and indulge lower-nature reactions.

Second, most situations we encounter require from us some adaptation, change, intervention, or adjustment to resolve them. Our tools for accomplishing this are thought and action, sometimes aided by higher "soul emotion." Lower-nature agitation, by contrast, is an "anti-tool": not only does it contribute nothing to the resolution process, it is an obstacle to it, as it interferes with thought and action and makes them more difficult. For example, consider the situation of having a flat tire. Resolving this situation requires only a small number of thoughts and actions. To change the tire ourselves, we have to either know how to do it (a group of thoughts) or open our car's owner's manual and read some simple instructions (thoughts expressed in writing or pictures), then execute them (actions). To get someone else to do it, we have to decide (thoughts) whom to ask—service station, auto club, friend, etc.—then call them (action). These simple thoughts and actions alone are what eventually result in the flat being fixed. Note that lower-nature agitation—feelings like fear, anger, anxiety, or frustration—does not understand flats and cannot fix them, so it adds nothing helpful to the process. But it does subtract valuable faculties and harm our efforts:

- It hinders clear thinking (analyzing, troubleshooting, problem-solving).
- It paralyzes our will and makes decisive action harder and less efficient.
- It drains us of energy that could be directed to dealing with the flat.
- It makes our life thoroughly miserable while we are fixing the flat.

Of course, many of the situations that we must deal with are far more difficult and demanding than having a flat tire. But no matter how serious or important a situation is, the fact is that it is always better for us—more practical, more efficient, more pleasant—to meet that situation without agitation than with it.

So how exactly do we stop shooting ourselves in the foot by unnecessarily adding lower reactions to already-trying situations? The crucial first step is the simple act of employing our imagination. At the moment when a situation arises, we must imagine the possibility of the situation existing, but of us not reacting. This may sound easy, but we will likely find that our conditioning militates against it. Years of experiencing situations and agitation arising in tandem will have left most of us with a habit of conceiving of the two as inseparable, and accepting that notion as a fact. This mind-set then effectively blocks our imagination from functioning: it simply "never occurs to us"—i.e., we never imagine—that things could be any other way.

To counteract this effect of our conditioning, we must "manually" activate our imagination in a new direction, picturing that it is quite possible to experience each situation that arises, and deal with it perfectly well and successfully, without having any lower-nature reactions layered onto it. The revised version of our earlier table, found on the following page, illustrates what we have to do.

What we are in effect prescribing is *to use our imagination in the service of our higher nature*. In the past, most of our active imaginings have probably centered on our lower nature and its desires and passions, and far fewer on our higher nature—as for instance imagining ourselves more benevolent or tolerant or fearless. Now we must begin consciously to employ our imagination in this latter way, as a bridge to our higher qualities—in this case, a calm and serene attitude toward worldly circumstances and events. The coming chapters (4–11) will describe in detail the specific techniques for achieving this goal of a dispassionate response to situations. But all of them require for their propulsion the basic factor of an active imagination directed towards the higher nature. Let us not underestimate the creative power of imagination to open doors. Just as envisioning an upcoming meal can produce immediate effects in our body, so also can directing our imagination toward new dispassion possibilities do the same in our psyche.

The thought of possibilities is already an opened path.—*Aum, 278*

If a person imagines in his thought that he has a certain quality, he is half way to possessing that quality; if he imagines himself free from a certain failing, he is half way to being free from it.—*The Mental Body,* 150–51.

Imagination is the eye of the soul.—Joseph Joubert

The ideal of the Spiritual can penetrate only through the imagination.— *Letters From the Masters of Wisdom, Second Series,* 41.

Sample Choices + New Possibilities

Choice #1: Situation	Choice #2: Situation + Problem	Imagination Activated: Situation − Problem
Have a flat tire	~~Have a flat tire, plus feel angry~~	It is possible to have a flat tire and not feel angry.
Friend never arrives for lunch date	~~Friend never arrives for lunch date, plus feel hurt~~	It is possible to have friend never arrive for lunch date and not feel hurt.
Fired from job	~~Fired from job, plus feel humiliated.~~	It is possible to be fired and not feel humiliated.
Late to work & hit every red light	~~Late to work & hit every red light, plus feel irritated~~	It is possible to be late to work & hit every red light and not feel irritated.
Son makes an "F" in math	~~Son makes an "F" in math, plus feel frustrated & embarrassed~~	It is possible to have son make an "F" and not feel frustrated & embarrassed.
Flight is canceled	~~Flight is canceled, plus feel furious~~	It is possible to have cancelled flight & not feel furious.
Rains on the day of picnic.	~~Rains on the day of picnic, plus feel bitter~~	It is possible to have rain on picnic day & not feel bitter.

D. The New Dispassion Ideal

In the past, most of us have held the conventional view that lower-nature agitation was caused by outer situations, and our goal was to evade what difficult situations we could, and suffer through our emotional reactions to those we could not. This view carried with it no overriding idea that such reactions were undesirable or that mastering them was a priority (or even a possibility). In fact, we may have even considered them good and necessary! For example, if someone verbally attacked us, our ideal response might have been to rush out and heatedly defend or explain ourselves; not doing so (we might have believed) would have resulted in a defeat, made us a loser, and rightly diminished our self-esteem and value. It would not have mattered that we became wildly agitated during this defense and felt miserable for hours afterwards, because preventing those effects was not part of our philosophy of how to respond.

Now, however, we have a new view of problems and situations, and with it comes a new, higher ideal that supersedes and must supplant the old one: *in all situations, we win when we meet them without becoming agitated.* This is now our highest priority and new standard of success, and it takes precedence over everything else. The following passage neatly captures this new ideal and standard:

> There was an ancient game in which people tried to make each other angry. Whoever became angry first was the loser.—*Brotherhood*, p. 31

Substitute any lower-nature quality for "angry" and we have a yardstick for measuring our approach to the dispassion ideal in any situation. That means that now if we rush out and heatedly defend and explain ourselves as in the old days, we lose. Note that it is not the defense or explanation that causes the defeat; we can defend and explain or not, as we see fit. Rather, it is the "heatedly" bit—the agitation we permit to accompany it. Thus does the new ideal focus our attention on the actual problem and point the way to solving it.

E. The Dispassion Principles in Action

Successfully adopting the new view of problems and situations laid out in this chapter results in radical changes in how we think, act, and live our daily lives. The changes in thinking manifest as (1) a new attitude and (2) a new guiding ideal or standard of success; in acting, as (3) a new way of meeting and dealing with situations. Each of these areas requires of us new efforts and new energy-management methods, so that we are always acting in our higher interest.

Let us illustrate these methods in action through a thought-experiment example. Suppose we were clairvoyant and could peek into both the exterior and interior life of a person—we will call her Robin—who understands the principles in this chapter, has successfully adopted the new views, and is trying to put them into practice. Here is what we might see in each area.

Robin is plagued by various unconquered lower-nature tendencies and often encounters situations that provoke a reaction from one of them. Today she opens a letter from her son's school and finds his report card. At that moment, a friend stops by to visit and notices that she is agitated, and the following conversation ensues. An analysis of how the PLS views each line in the dialogue is in brackets and italics:

> F: What's wrong? [*i.e., What problem do you have?*]
> R: I'm angry and frustrated. [*Correctly identifies the problem*]
> F: What made you angry? [*Expresses old view of problems*]
> R: I did. [*Asserts new view of problems*]
> F: But I see you looking at an "F" on your son's report card. [*Suggests that the "F" is the real problem and "caused" the anger*]
> R: Yes, but that's irrelevant. I'm the one making me angry, and I know how to stop it. [*Refuses to blame provoking agent, reasserts true nature of problem, prepares to use dispassion techniques*]
> F: Huh? [*Friend obviously not a PLS user*]

The friend soon leaves, and Robin is alone. When she again contemplates the "F" on the report card, we observe a surge of instinctive agitation in her psyche: frustration, anger, disappointment, disbelief, etc. She realizes that this situation is a difficult provocation and represents a major challenge to her new attitude, which she feels already beginning to slip. So she pauses, and we see her remove from her purse a reminder checklist [facing page] that she has made for herself for just such occasions. [Note: this checklist and subsequent ones found at the end of the next eight chapters are available to download as printable pdf's from www.thepls.org.]

> **My "New Dispassion Attitude" Checklist**
> - All my problems are the result of agitation of my own lower nature.
> - When I am thrown into agitation, it is my own fault—always.
> - No person/thing is "making" me feel or think anything—nor can they.
> - Whatever I feel or think, I and I alone am making me feel or think it.
> - I can prevent/remove problems by applying the dispassion techniques.
> - To do this, I direct my attention within, to the source of the problem.
> - I refuse to focus attention outward on what provokes any problem.
> - I refuse self-pity, indignation, criticism, or blame of any outer factor.
> - Thus I can solve each problem quickly and efficiently, with the least harm to myself and others who may inadvertently provoke me.
> - As a result, I remain calm, centered, and dispassionate in any situation.

Consulting the list restores and fortifies Robin's attitude, which now acts as a shield and checks the surging lower energy. This leaves her mind calm and able to think clearly. She remembers that although this is a situation she must deal with decisively, she can do so dispassionately. She activates her imagination and pictures to herself how this is possible. She then analyzes the situation and considers the various ways she can deal with it:

- I can talk to my son about his grade—but without being agitated.
- I can have a conference with his teacher—but without being agitated.
- I can get him a tutor—but without being agitated.
- I can try to make him study more—but without being agitated.
- I can restrict his freedom if necessary—but without being agitated.

She affirms that each of these actions addresses the situation (the "F"), yet leaves her without a problem (frustration, anger, disappointment, etc.). And to prevent future agitation in this matter, she notes to herself:

> It is possible that none of these actions will work, and my son will fail his class and have to retake it. But if he does, he can fail without my being agitated, and he can retake it without my being agitated. Whatever happens, I can do my best to help him, but while not being agitated. This is the ideal I strive to live up to. Each time I do so, I win a satisfying victory over my lower nature, and I'm happier and freer; each time I don't, I foolishly hurt my own self, and I'm unhappy and mired in bondage.

F. Summary

- We can view the cause of our problems in two opposing ways:
  - They are caused by people, events, and circumstances outside us.
  - They are caused by lower-nature energies within us.
- To practice dispassion, we adopt the "caused-by-lower-nature" view.
- Outer situations emanate no rays that make us think/feel anything.
- Outer situations may provoke agitation, but they do not cause it.
- Outer situations are ultimately irrelevant to solving our problems.
- In all situations, we have two choices:
  - Have the situation.
  - Have the situation, plus be thrown into agitation about it.
- Practicing dispassion demands that we reject "situation-plus-agitation."
  - It is against our higher interest.
  - It makes it harder to address and deal with the situation.
- It is possible to have any situation without layering agitation onto it.
- Separating situations from agitation requires using our imagination.
- The new view of situations/problems includes with it a new ideal.
- Our new ideal: we win when we meet situations without agitation.
- This new ideal is our top priority and ultimate standard of success.
- The table on the facing page summarizes the science of dispassion.

The Science of Dispassion: Summary

	Old View	New View
Underlying Philosophy	Everyone and everything outside myself have the power to agitate me.	No people or things outside myself have the power to agitate me, even if they desired.
Source of Problems	All my problems come from the outside world.	All my problems come from within myself.
Number of Problems to Address	My problems are unlimited, because an infinite number of people and circumstances can "cause" them.	I have only one problem—my own psyche and its lower-nature contents.
Prospects for Locating and Solving Problems	I cannot permanently solve problems because they are located "out there"; if "solved" on one front, they soon reappear on another.	I am assured of eventually solving all problems because I have accurately identified, and work within, the realm where they exist (my psyche).
Examples of use of *make* in sentences	She makes me angry. He makes me afraid. They make me depressed. It makes me give up.	She makes me a résumé. He makes me a sandwich. Poison ivy makes me itch. I make me worried.
Effects on Thought-Life	Thought-energy is readily used to support self-pity, indignation, a sense of injustice, and criticism/blame of others. Thus few mental resources remain to address the real problem.	No thought-energy is wasted to support self-pity, indignation, a sense of injustice, or criticism/blame of others. Thus the full resources of my mind are available for addressing the real problem.
Ideal	Getting agitated when misunderstood/ attacked is good & necessary as an incentive to explaining/defending myself. If I do not do this, I am defeated and a loser and rightly diminished in my self-value or self-esteem.	Getting agitated is never in my higher interest, because the moment my mind & emotions become agitated, they can no longer register my higher nature. It is when I'm not thrown into agitation that I'm a winner and victor.
Standard for Success	I win when I get agitated & defend & explain myself, even though as a result I become inflamed and feel horrible.	I win when I am not thrown into agitation, whatever the provocation; so I feel good no matter what happens.

We have now completed our survey of the principles underlying the practice of dispassion and are ready to begin studying the specific individual techniques listed below. Used together, these techniques will remove the primary causes of most of the lower-nature agitation that afflicts us.

- Seeking and accepting facts without wishing they were different
- Expecting nothing from any person, event, or circumstance
- Rejecting seriousness of the wrong kind
- Learning through experimentation
- Minding our own business
- Curbing needless speculation
- Forgetting the past
- Controlling speech

All these techniques are designed as preventives and therefore work best when applied *in advance* of situations likely to provoke lower reactions. Most of us already manage the physical events of our daily lives in this way. For example, when taking a trip, we consult a map and plan our route beforehand to avoid needless trouble. Practicing dispassion requires the same kind of preparation for psychological events. When we know, for instance, that we are soon to encounter Person A or Situation B, we must choose which dispassion techniques will prevent whatever agitation we anticipate, then apply them. (Step-by-step suggestions and experiments are included with each technique.)

For situations that are not foreseeable or of unpredictable character, we must have the techniques at our fingertips and apply them on the fly. If doing that fails to work, some of the techniques can be used afterwards to help us silence the agitation and understand better how to prevent it in the future. But the ideal is to use all of them in advance rather than for damage control.

4

SEEKING & ACKNOWLEDGING FACTS

A. The Problem

Inherent in all people and situations that we encounter and interact with is a set of facts about their nature, character, history, purposes, etc. Unfortunately, we often find ourselves living at odds—or even at war—with many of these facts. This mismatch is usually traceable to three simple causes:

- We fail to look for facts about people or situations.
- We fail to acknowledge/accept facts when we find them.
- We fail to stop wishing/hoping that the facts were different from what they are.

Here are examples from ordinary speech, followed in brackets by the "fact-trouble" they represent:

"I had no idea that my husband would play video games every night."
[But the fact is, before you were married he behaved in just this way in your presence many times.]

"It's hard to accept that Susan lied to me; she's an honest person."
[But the fact is, she lied at least once, so she is not 100% honest.]

"The people sitting behind us should not be talking during the movie."
[But the fact is, the people sitting behind you *are* talking, despite what you believe they should or should not do.]

"It's not fair that the company promoted Scott and not me."
[But the fact is, they *did* promote Scott, regardless of if it was fair.]

"I wish it weren't so cold."
[But the fact is, it *is* cold, and your wishing will not change that.]

"I hope the X-ray doesn't show that I have a broken arm."
[But the fact is, your arm already *is* either broken or not, and your hoping will not change whichever it is.]

Whatever the cause—obliviousness, denial, wishful thinking, beliefs, codes of conduct—walking around out of sync with facts is a major enemy of dispassion. It sets up a perpetual conflict in our psyche and results in all manner of lower-nature feeling-agitation when the facts inevitably assert themselves: anger, resentment, criticism, self-pity, futility, dissatisfaction, disappointment. It also agitates our mind with endless movie loops in which images of what we believed or wished the facts were, repeatedly collide with images of the facts as they actually are. And if producing all this agitation were not enough, it is also draining. Fueling and maintaining a war with facts requires a constant expenditure of energy that could be spent on more elevating pursuits—like seeking facts and adjusting to them. Instead, the resulting energy depletion leaves us less able to oppose our lower reactions and more likely to be sucked into their downward spiral.

In addition to being an enemy of dispassion, failing to seek and accept facts is an affront to truth. Our higher nature is inherently rational, discriminating, honest, and truthful; the coin of its realm is facts, steadily sought and calmly accepted. By contrast, the lower nature consists of countless irrational agitations that are unrelated to truth and do not seek or value it. Under the latter's influence, we indiscriminately allow into our mind unvetted thoughts and ideas that masquerade as facts and truth, instead of using our higher-nature faculties to investigate, inquire, research, and discriminate about them. The following passage clearly lays out the problem:

> You must distinguish between truth and falsehood; you must learn to be true all through—in thought, word, and deed. In thought first; and that is not easy, for there are in the world many untrue thoughts, many foolish superstitions, and no one who is enslaved by them can make progress. Therefore you must not hold a thought just because many other people hold it, nor because it has been believed for centuries, nor because it is written in some book which people hold sacred; you must think of the matter for yourself, and judge for yourself whether it is reasonable. ... He who would walk upon the Path must learn to think for himself, for superstition is one of the greatest evils in the world, one of the fetters from which you must utterly free yourself.—Alcyone (J. Krishnamurti), *At the Feet of the Master*, 4.

This problem of truth and falsity extends to our relations with others as well. The trouble begins when we do not even bother to investigate what people are really like, or we reject the facts we see about them, but instead walk around with images and notions of them that we have invented without any regard for their accuracy. As a result, we interact not with the real people before us, but with the private, false replicas of them that we have conjured in our mind—hardly a recipe for good communication or good relationships. Even worse, we may judge them and gossip about them based on our incorrect notions, spreading false information and causing confusion and pain. This kind of callous disrespect and disregard for truth is doubly harmful: not only does every instance of it unfairly make others' lives harder, but it simultaneously drags us down into our lower nature and withers our connection with our higher nature.

B. The Solution

Eliminating trouble with facts is simply a matter of reversing the three failings outlined at the beginning of this chapter, so that you:

- Search diligently for the facts about people or situations.
- Accept the facts without reservation when you find them.
- Refuse to wish or hope that the facts were different from what they are.

Below are the PLS methods for implementing them. The first seven constitute the ideal sequence to follow; the last two describe difficulties that often disrupt it.

Become an active fact-finder and truth-seeker.

A surprising number of people fail at this simple task, for various reasons: laziness, failure to pay attention, failure to search in the right way or in the right places, lack of awareness of how much trouble their ignorance might cause them, and so on. Here are two examples:

> "Gosh, I had no idea that Natalie was so unhappy in her marriage that she would get a divorce."
> [Then you must have missed the thousand clues in her speech, body language, facial expressions, emotional reactions, criticisms, complaints, etc., over the last decade.]

"I just realized that ever since I was young, when people criticize me, even constructively, I am defensive and hostile and secretly mad at them for days."
[Then you must have been insufficiently attentive to this inner commotion that has repeatedly arisen in your psyche, each time causing painful lower-nature agitation and relationship conflicts.]

The remedy for such failures is simply to start paying attention to the situations and people you encounter outside you, and the higher- and lower-nature energies that arise within you.

Use effective fact-searching methods.

In general, facts are found most quickly and efficiently through the methods in the left column of the table below. (For contrast, their opposites are in the right column.)

Fact-Finding Tools	**Fact-Finding Enemies**
Listening	Talking
Asking questions	Making statements
Observing	Disregarding, ignoring
Questioning your beliefs	Asserting your beliefs
Questioning all your thoughts	Believing all your thoughts
Opening your mind	Closing your mind
Experimenting	Speculating, guessing
Suspending/delaying judgment	Jumping to conclusions

These common-sense tools are hardly a mystery; after all, they are the same ones used every day by scientists across the world. For the PLS user, the task is to realize that they can be used in every area of life, and to develop the habit of doing so. Suppose, for instance, that your boss says something that you find confusing or alarming. Instead of speculating that she is upset with you, or jumping to the conclusion that she is, simply ask her, "What did you mean by X?" or "Are you dissatisfied with me or my work?" By responding in this way, you are likely to discover the actual facts, as well as avoid painful lower reactions that would inevitably accompany your non-fact-seeking. Note that to get the most complete and truthful answers when you question others, be sure to create an atmosphere in which they feel safe to be entirely candid. This means promising them that they need not fear that you will judge or punish them for what they think or feel—*and meaning it!* Nothing poisons communication and relationships more than demanding that people tell the truth, then punishing them (openly or subtly) for doing so.

Understand what the PLS means by "accept the facts."

In the PLS, "accept the facts" means simply "acknowledge or admit the existence of the facts we encounter." In doing this, we are not condoning the facts, but merely recognizing them for what they are at that moment—a necessary prelude for dealing with them effectively and dispassionately. Therefore, it does not mean "tolerate or accommodate ourselves to some condition or activity that the facts describe," as many facts are reprehensible and intolerable, like racism or child abuse outside us, or fear and hatred within us. Our higher nature demands that we not regard these as "acceptable," but rather work vigorously, though dispassionately, to change them.

Insist on intellectual honesty.

Develop the integrity to set aside all your personal ideas, beliefs, concepts, prejudices, wishes, feelings, motives, etc., when they clash with the truth or facts that your searching reveals. In other words, be intellectually honest. That means respecting evidence, refusing to rationalize or spin the facts to match your preconceptions about them, and acknowledging that your ideas are wrong when the facts show them to be so.

In addition to admitting objective facts, intellectual honesty also includes refusing to invent imaginary ones. During a typical day, thousands of thoughts will arise in your mind. Many of them, especially those provoked by lower-nature agitation, are simply not true. Therefore, adopt a healthy skepticism toward all thoughts and scrutinize them carefully. Instead of automatically believing them, ask yourself, "Is this thought true? Do I really know it is true? Or did my mind just invent this idea with no rational basis or evidence?"

Activate your accept-the-facts imagination.

Once you have found and acknowledged a fact, do whatever is necessary to wholeheartedly accept it. With many facts, this is no problem: you easily adjust your concepts to accommodate them, and move on. With others, however, it may be harder (see "Beware of denial" below). For these cases, your primary weapon to overcome mental resistance is imagination, and you can use it in several ways to oppose any obstacle. You can first try simply imagining yourself accepting the facts; often this alone is enough to jar loose any resistance. You can imagine all the harm and suffering that refusing to accept them could cause you and others in the future. You can imagine the revision of your idea of a person or situation (or yourself) that makes it match the new facts you have acknowledged. Finally, you can imagine yourself devising a solution to the problems the facts create, then executing it. But however you accomplish it, you must ultimately accept facts, as in the end it is futile and self-defeating to set yourself against them. As the economist John Maynard Keynes is reputed to have put it, "When the facts change, I change my mind. What do you do, sir?"

Strive for the maximum adaptability and flexibility.

When you drive a car, you make continuous, rapid adjustments as the facts before you change. You never think, "I shouldn't have to switch lanes because that car pulled out in front of me," and then not switch lanes; or, "I wish that light ahead hadn't turned red," and then drive through it. Instead, you act on your higher interest and immediately switch lanes or stop at the light in response to the changed facts, whether you like them or not. In acting thus, you prevent no end of trouble, pain, and suffering for yourself and your fellow drivers.

You can train yourself to make the same immediate adjustments in every other area of life, with the same benefits. So once you recognize the existence of a fact, try to accept it instantly. Make a game of seeing just how fast you can adjust your concepts, ideas, images, notions, beliefs, etc.—or even discard them entirely—when you discover that they do not match facts you have encountered. The ultimate goal is to turn on a dime, shrinking the time between when you realize a truth or fact, and when you accept it, to zero. This rapid adjustment serves two purposes: it prevents creating a time-gap between acceptance and adjustment in which anti-dispassion mischief can occur, and it quickly moves your attention to the task of how best to respond to the changed facts.

Refuse to wish the accepted facts were different from what they are.
Once you have succeeded in finding and accepting facts, be careful not to sabotage the process by failing at this one last requirement, like this:

> Mary wants a certain degree from a university. She investigates and finds that to get it, she must take a series of required courses. She accepts this fact, enrolls in the courses, and attends class. But every day, she wishes that she did not have to take these particular classes, resents having to do so, and complains to everyone about the fact.

Practicing dispassion demands that along with going to class and doing the work, Mary must stop indulging both thoughts of wishing that she did not have to do this and lower-nature reactions to such wishes. If she does not, all her efforts to live dispassionately and avoid agitation go up in smoke.

Note that one kind of wishful thinking can be constructive and helpful—when it expresses a desire to change something that (1) can be changed and (2) the changing of which would improve your life. For instance, thinking, "I wish I ate a more healthful diet," could inspire a series of beneficent actions: researching which foods to eliminate and add, finding new recipes, buying the new foods, and establishing the habit of eating them. When thinking like this can further your higher interest, of course use it to the full. But always refuse to indulge the more common, harmful type described above—wishing to change something that you cannot change.

The process we have just described of interacting with and internalizing facts should ideally be one smooth, uninterrupted sequence:

seek facts => find facts => accept facts => adjust/respond to facts

Trouble arises when the forward motion of this sequence is disrupted by lower-nature reactions, typically these:

> ... find facts -> *resist or deny facts* => accept facts ...
> ... accept facts => *stew about facts* => adjust to facts ...

Let us analyze each.

Beware of denial.
We all create mental images or interior replicas of the situations and people (including ourselves) in our world. It is human nature to project

onto certain of these replicas our own powerful hopes and desires. If we happen to be very attached to such a replica, but encounter painful facts that do not match it, we may find ourselves rejecting or denying those facts despite our best efforts to be honest with ourselves. Here is an example:

> Despite indisputable daily evidence in the bathroom, Don and Glenda insist that their daughter does not have bulimia, because they think of her as far too smart and "together" for that.

Not only does denying facts that they know deep down are true saddle Don and Glenda with continuous, nagging agitation and foreboding, but it could also result in serious medical problems for their daughter. Clearly, denial like this is in no one's higher interest. So be alert to signs of it in yourself, like a strong desire that the facts be a certain way, or a great resistance to them, or a tendency to make up your own "facts" when you do not like the real ones. If you do find yourself resisting or denying, remember that imagination is the tool of choice for overcoming it.

Resist the urge to delay accepting a fact and instead stew about it.

The antithesis of rapid adaptability is an attitude of perverse resistance that keeps us beating our head against a wall over a fact and refusing to accept it. Most often, we fall into the "stewing trap" because of either strongly-held codes of conduct (what should/should not happen, what is/is not fair) or our misuse of the natural human desire to know why (why something is happening, why someone did something). If you find yourself indignantly and heatedly using any of the phrases below, you may have fallen into this trap:

> What kind of person would _____ ?! No one should _____ !
> I don't understand why _____ ! It's not fair that _____ !

Here are two typical examples, with the keywords in italics:

> Marilyn strongly believes that people should not talk in theaters during movies. She goes to a movie where other patrons are talking, a fact she passionately refuses to accept: "All these people *shouldn't be* talking during the movie! People *ought to be* more considerate! *What kind of manager would* tolerate this? It's *not fair!*"

> Bill drives to a store to buy an Acme drill and has this exchange with a clerk:

C: I'm sorry, sir, we're out of Acme drills.
B: (agitated) What?! *Why* are you out?
C: Uh, people bought all of them.
B: Well *why* didn't you order more of them to start with?
C: I don't know, sir, I'm not the buyer. Would you like a different brand?
B: But you advertised them! *Why* do that and then run out?

Practicing dispassion demands that instead of stewing in agitation over "should not," "not fair," and "why," Marilyn and Bill must calmly note and accept the facts, then promptly move on to planning and executing a response to the situation they create. In Marilyn's case, she could ask the talkers to stop; complain to the manager; move to a seat where she cannot hear the talking; stop going to theaters to see movies —anything but sit there and agitate herself over a fact. For Bill, he could try this alternate version of his conversation which bypasses all the unnecessary why's:

C: I'm sorry, sir, we're out of Acme drills.
B: Oh, no! ... Well, when will you have more?
C: They're supposed to arrive Tuesday.
B: OK. What's your number, so I can call ahead to be sure they're here?

By responding thus, Bill prevents agitation, advances his purpose of buying a drill, and kindly avoids delaying the customers behind him. And if he is one of the many people particularly plagued by a "why-function" run amok, he might pause and contemplate the great freedom that results from simply letting most things be as they are, without demanding to know why and burdening himself with needless information.

Note that in recommending these actions, the PLS does not deny that certain things ought to be one way instead of another, or that certain things are indeed unfair, or that it can be important to know why certain things happen. It merely maintains that they must not interfere with or trump the dispassion practice of calmly accepting facts and calmly dealing with them.

C. Exercises for Accepting Facts

The following exercises are based on all the principles discussed above and address both general and specific topics.

General exercise for accepting facts
- Recall how living out of sync with facts causes lower-nature agitation.
  - It sets up a perpetual conflict in your psyche.
  - It results in feeling-agitation when facts thwart your desires and wishes.
  - It agitates the mind when non-factual inner images collide with outer facts.
  - These reactions create needless stress and drain you of energy.
- Note that such reactions are self-created and your responsibility.
  - They are caused by you, the non-acceptor of facts.
  - They are not caused by the person or situation the facts were about.
- Note that such reactions do not serve your higher interest.
  - Consider the (self-inflicted) harm they can cause you.
  - Consider the harm they can cause others.
- *Then imagine it is possible to accept any fact without being agitated..*
  - "I can accept whatever X is like without being agitated about it."
  - "I can accept whatever Y does without being agitated about it."
  - "I can accept however Z is organized without being agitated about it."
  - "And nothing is stopping me from accepting these facts immediately."
- Note the many beneficial effects of this imagining on how you feel.
  - More peace—no longer at war with any facts
  - Less clutter—mind is free of fact-contrary thoughts that take up space
  - More clarity—can see things as they are and be more objective
  - More energy—don't waste your forces waging a war with facts
  - More integrity—honor facts/truth over personal opinions/motives.
  - More productivity—get things done instead of complaining about facts.
  - More freedom—not imprisoned by and dragged down by falsehoods.

Exercise for investigating the truth of thoughts
- Identify thoughts or lines of thought of questionable veracity.
- If necessary for clarity, write them down.
- Then take each thought and ask yourself:
  - Is this thought actually true? Do I really know it's true?
  - Is there a rational basis or evidence for believing it?
  - Have I sought and confirmed facts to support it?
  - Or did it in fact arise from feeling-agitation, or hunger, or hormones?
- Imagine how you could verify or confirm the thought.
  - "I could ask Person X whether she feels what I think she feels."
  - "I could research Situation Y to learn if it really is as I think it is."
  - "I could ask Person Z if his actions meant what I think they meant."
- Imagine thereby learning facts and adjusting your ideas to match them.
- Imagine the benefits this would produce for you and others.
  - Your mind would be free of falsehoods.
  - You would relate to others based more closely on who they actually are.
  - You would interact with situations free from false conceptions about them.

D. Seeking & Accepting Facts in Action

Now let us continue our thought experiment involving our friend Robin—whom we met at the end of the previous chapter—to see how she applies the accept-the-facts techniques to her situation with her son. When she contemplates the "F" on his report card, we see the surge of agitation in her psyche (frustration, anger, disappointment), which in turn provokes disbelief and wild thoughts:

> What? An F?! This cannot be! My son is not a F-student; he has never made an F before. I have a Master's degree, for Pete's sake; no son of mine should be making F's! That's just not who he is! … I just hope this isn't true. … Oh, no, suppose this is the start of a downward spiral. He could fail out of school and never get a job and end up in prison or living under a bridge. And it's all my fault for not making sure he did his homework.

Observing this barrage of thoughts, Robin recognizes that she has a "fact" problem. So she consults a checklist she has made for herself:

My "Accept the Facts" Checklist

- Am I actively seeking the facts?
    - Paying attention to outer situations/people & my inner psyche?
    - Asking questions? Listening? Not jumping to conclusions?
- Am I acknowledging and accepting the facts when I find them?
    - Being honest with myself about my beliefs vs. facts I discover?
    - Questioning the truth of my thoughts and not inventing facts?
    - Using my imagination to accept the facts wholeheartedly?
    - Changing my mind & adapting to facts as soon as I find them?
- Am I refusing to wish or hope that the facts are different?
- Am I being vigilant against denial?
- Am I refusing to stew about facts because of *should*, *fair*, or *why*?

This review orients Robin to the problem and calms her mind, and she notes to herself:

> No, I am not actively seeking the facts about the F, I'm just reacting. No, I have questioned no one to discover the facts. Yes, I feel resistance to accepting facts that clash with my image of my son. No, I am not questioning whether all my wild thoughts are true. Yes, I am hoping that the F isn't true, even though it wastes energy and changes nothing.

Yes, I am stewing because of "should" instead of getting the facts and addressing the situation they create. It is clearly in my higher interest to change all this.

With her problem clarified to herself, Robin makes a few phone calls and determines that the "F" is real, that her son is mortified about it and determined to change it, and that his teacher has suggestions about how best to address it. Armed with these facts, Robin does a short accept-the-facts exercise. We observe her thoughts:

My son made an F; it's an undeniable fact that I must accept. ... [Tries to imagine integrating this fact into her image of her son and her own self-image. Meets resistance.] If I don't do this, it will only hurt both of us: it will keep me stewing in agitation, and it will interfere with my getting him the help he needs. ... [Imagines him getting help and righting his ship. Her agitation begins to subside.] ... OK, no need to waste another second resisting; he made the "F," it's a fact, I accept it, done. ... Ah, peace again!

Her psyche back in adjustment, Robin is now free to act decisively to address this new and (to her) unfamiliar situation.

E. Summary

- We often find ourselves in conflict with the facts around us.
- This conflict is usually due to three causes:
    - Fail to look for facts about people or situations
    - Fail to acknowledge/accept facts when we find them
    - Fail to stop wishing/hoping facts were different from what they are
- Living out of sync with facts is a major enemy of dispassion.
    - It agitates our emotions and mind.
    - It drains us through a constant, needless expenditure of energy.
- Failing to seek and accept facts is an affront to truth.
    - Our higher nature values facts, steadily sought/calmly accepted.
    - Our lower nature has no relation to truth/does not seek or value it.
    - It permits unvetted thoughts that masquerade as facts and truth.
    - It does not investigate, inquire, research, discriminate about them.
- Failing to seek and accept facts mars our relations with others.
    - We do not interact with the real people before us.
    - We interact with false mental replicas of them we privately invent.

- Solving fact-trouble requires reversing the three usual failings:
  - Search diligently for the facts about people or situations.
  - Accept the facts without reservation when you find them.
  - Refuse to wish that the facts were different from what they are.
- The PLS uses six methods for accomplishing this:
  - Become an active fact-finder and truth-seeker.
  - Use effective fact-searching methods (ask, listen, observe, etc.).
  - Be intellectually honest: accept evidence and do not invent facts.
  - Activate your accept-the-facts imagination.
  - Adjust to each fact as quickly as possible.
  - Waste no energy wishing the new facts were otherwise.
- "Seek facts => find facts => accept facts => adjust/respond to facts."
- Refuse to indulge in denial of facts.
- Resist the urge to delay accepting a fact in order to stew about it.
  - Stewing often arises from codes of conduct (should, ought, fair).
  - Stewing often arises from needless insistence on knowing "why."

5

EXPECTING NOTHING

A. The Problem

Expectations are ideas or beliefs that we create about people, circumstances, and events. Here are examples from a variety of situations ranging from superficial to profound:

I am expecting that…

- the person I invited to lunch will show up.
- my child will not embarrass me by getting arrested for shoplifting.
- other people will understand me and my motives.
- I will not be unfairly fired from my job.
- what my parents taught me is true.
- the person I'm doing business with will honor the contract we signed.
- my spouse or partner will be faithful to me.
- my good friends will never lie to me or deceive me.
- someone will be there for me when I am confused or hurting.
- I will never become disillusioned with my teacher/mentor/guru.
- everyone I love will still be alive when I wake up tomorrow.

Although we may not like to think about it, most of us are aware that there is no guarantee of anything in earth life, and thus we have no real basis for counting on expectations like the ones above with absolute certainty—especially when they involve human nature or human events or interactions with other human personalities. Given this fact, as long as we treat our expectations strictly as "things likely to happen—but they might not," they pose no danger. But the moment we cross the line and start regarding them as "things we can rely on, count on, depend on happening—and they had better happen or we will be really upset," we have bought ourselves a ticket to dispassion disaster. For every expectation of this latter type is a psychological land mine that we lay in our own psyche, and eventually some person (or situation) will "step on" one, and it will blow up. One day our friend does *not* show up for our lunch date, or we *are* fired from our job, or our child *is* arrested for shoplifting, or any other of a million things we created expectations about and staked our happiness and well-being on. The resulting explosion—which takes place of course in *our* psyche—unleashes toxic agitation: irritation and criticism at our no-show friend, resentment and anger at the company that fired us, panic and disillusion at our arrested child. *And all this is our own fault*, since it was we who invented the expectations and decided to treat them as a sure thing. Of course, we still have to deal with whatever situations arise, but layering onto them agitation caused by expectations that we know, deep down, are ultimately unenforceable, is self-defeating and against our higher interest.

It is bad enough that creating expectations harms ourselves, but doing so also leads us to harm others by making demands of them, then subtly (or openly) punishing them for not fulfilling these demands. Imagine how this appears and feels from their point of view. They are minding their own business and living the best they can when, unbeknownst to them and without any consultation with them, we make up an expectation about how they should be and what they should do. Then, in some innocent interaction with us, they find themselves the unhappy recipient first of the demand we radiate at them based on our private expectation, then of our disapproval and criticism when they fail to fulfill it. This is nothing less than an unfair "energy-attack" on them, which by no standard could be considered anything other than rude and inconsiderate.

And this is not just any ordinary rudeness either, like failing to be outwardly polite and say "please" and "thank you." Rather, it is an egregious violation of what I call "soul courtesy," the true inner courtesy that is inherent in our higher nature and extended to all our fellow souls. It is based on the heart-knowledge that nature has endowed all humans with the freedom to live and experiment in the way they think best for them, as they struggle to find, be, and express their best self. Knowing that such a process is difficult for everyone, soul courtesy thus scrupulously avoids actions that infringe others' free will or unfairly make their lives harder—like making up expectations about them, insisting that they fulfill them, and punishing them when they do not.

Now if expectations are so detrimental to our higher interest, why then do we habitually create so many of them? The answer is often traceable to the three major flaws in our relationship with facts that we studied in the previous chapter:

- Failing to look for facts about people or situations.
- Failing to accept facts when we find them.
- Failing to stop wishing facts were different from what they are.

For instance, we may invent the idea that our children or parents or co-workers are a certain way, or ought to be a certain way—honest and reliable, say—but make no effort to observe whether the facts of their conduct match our assumption. Or we may observe facts about them that are contrary to our idea of them, but dismiss those facts with thoughts like, "Well, even though they didn't tell the truth or do what they promised to do, they really *are* honest and reliable." Or we may note and accept the facts of instances of their dishonesty and unreliability, but indulge in endless wishing that they were not like that.

Once we do any of these things, it becomes easy to create expectations based on our own obliviousness, denial, or wishful thinking. Here is a typical sequence of thought:

> I *wish* Ann talked less. => She really *ought to* talk less. => Her talking really bothers me. => Surely I *have a right to expect* her to talk less. => She had better talk less. => If she doesn't, she'll pay for it.

In defiance of the fact that Ann is a person who talks a lot, we make up the wish-based expectation (lay the land mine in our psyche) that she will somehow suddenly stop being herself and start talking less. Then when she does not do this ("steps on" our land mine by talking), our expectation blows up in our face, and we become irritated, angry, resentful, intolerant, cruel, etc. Thus it is *we,* not Ann, who primarily "pay for it" through the agitation we suffer, although we may also do Ann the soul discourtesy of aiming our agitation at her for the "crime" of being herself.

Note that giving up wishful thinking (or obliviousness or denial, as the case may be) would eliminate any possibility of self-created trouble (and collateral damage to others):

> I wish Ann talked less, *but she doesn't.* (fact) => *Talking a lot is what she does.* (fact) => Therefore, I *won't be expecting* her to talk less. => If I need to not be around excessive talking, I will choose other company.

Now we have invented no expectation that is at war with the facts—a war we will never win and one opposed to our higher interest.

Clearly, then, expectations are a bad business for both ourselves and others. In my experience, they are the number one enemy of dispassion and the primary cause of self-inflicted misery in human life. Therefore, our higher interest demands that we cease creating and harboring them. Let us investigate how.

B. The Solution

If we have something that is causing us nothing but trouble, the obvious remedy is simply to get rid of it. As malignant psychological possessions, expectations clearly fall into this category. So we can state the solution to this problem in a single sentence:

Expect nothing from any person, event, or circumstance.

In theory, this is the only technique we need, and most of us will have no trouble applying it successfully—but only after we become aware of all our expectations and how they manifest. And therein lies the rub, because in practice most people at first fail to recognize the existence of the bulk of their expectations, as well as grossly underestimate the number of them. Therefore, in this section we will focus our attention on the principles and techniques necessary to gain a clear awareness of all our expectations, then follow with exercises which will make removing them relatively easy.

Recognize the different types of expectations.

Because expectations vary in the forms they assume and the process by which we create them, our awareness of them ranges from keenly conscious to blankly unconscious. Some expectations are explicit. If, say, you have a discussion with your spouse to clear up a conflict, the result might be, "From now on, you can expect X from me, and I can expect Y from you." The expectation thus created is clear, and you are fully aware of it.

Other expectations do not exist in such a definite form and in the forefront of our minds. For example, if you make a lunch date with a friend, you probably do not formulate the specific thought, "I expect that my friend will show up." But it is human nature simply to assume so, thus creating a kind of semi-conscious, background expectation.

Many ideals, beliefs, or codes of conduct are actually disguised forms of expectations—or only a step away from morphing into them. Suppose that you hold the belief, "Store clerks ought to be polite to customers." Such a belief can easily and unconsciously turn into, "I expect that store clerks will be polite to me." Or perhaps your idea of a friend is someone loyal, dependable, there when you need her, etc.—and you yourself always take care to be those things to others. This idea can then stealthily change into an expectation that people you label as "friends" will display those same qualities in their conduct toward you.

Using these categories as a guide, you can begin to inventory your psyche to see what expectations you can identify of each type.

Study each lower-nature agitation to see if it reveals an expectation.

When expectations are implicit or hidden or disguised as described above, we often discover their existence only when they manifest through a lower-nature reaction. Therefore, pay close attention to every reaction; they are your friend in the business of exposing expectations. As each arises, stop and ask yourself, "Is an expectation behind this thought or feeling?" To determine the answer, see if you can translate what you are thinking and feeling into "expectation format"—sentences like "I was expecting that..." or "Surely I had a right to expect that...." Then compare the facts about the translation with your original thought. Here are some examples:

Thought: My friend has promised to be on time.
Translation: Since she promised, surely I can expect she'll be on time.
Fact: But she's always late, so this expectation has no legitimate basis.

Thought: Teachers ought to know what they are doing.
Translation: I was expecting my teacher to know what he was doing.
Fact: Just because a person has the artificial title "Teacher" does not mean he knows what he is doing; he may or may not. Only his actions will tell.

Feeling: I feel hurt because my coworker criticized me.
Translation: I was expecting that my coworker would never criticize me.
Fact: But she has often criticized others, so why expect different about me?

Feeling: I feel angry at my husband for being insensitive.
Translation: My husband is family; family members should be sensitive to each other; surely I had a right to expect my husband not to be insensitive.
Fact: A person's being a member of a category (family) does not insure that he possesses a given quality (sensitivity). Only his actions show if he does.

Seek out expectations lurking in mundane situations.
  Another useful exercise is to pick some perfectly ordinary upcoming event and investigate what tacit expectations you have about it. In the case of, say, a dental appointment, you might uncover the following:

I am expecting that…
- the dentist's office told me the correct appointment time.
- the dentist will be at her office when I arrive.
- the dentist will see me at the time she said.
- the procedure described as routine, will be routine.
- I will be at the office for the amount of time the dentist told me.

Then note that although the above expectations may be likely, it is always possible that one or more of them could not happen:

- You arrive at the office and are informed that your appointment is two hours later, even though they told you it was now.
- You arrive at the office, and the dentist is gone and will not see you.
- The dentist sees you much later than she said.
- The "routine" procedure is anything but.
- The visit the dentist said would take ten minutes takes an hour.

(By the way, all of the above happened to a student I was tutoring. She had not studied the PLS and was mightily agitated.)

Once you find expectations, recall the "land mine" scenario.
  Expectations appear benign while lying quietly and calmly in some corner of your psyche. Therefore, it is necessary constantly to remind yourself of the pain and suffering their exploding will inevitably cause if you should leave them there and tempt fate to "step on" them. So as you discover each expectation that you are harboring, note what lower-nature agitations you leave yourself open to as long as it remains lying there, and why it is in your higher interest to remove it. Here are two examples of the thought process you might apply in given situations:

> I am expecting the customer service agent I'm about to talk to, to be polite, competent, and well-informed. If he's not, I would feel irritated and hostile. But then I would be agitated and miserable, and all because I was harboring this expectation and it exploded. Therefore, it is in my higher interest to remove it. I can still do whatever is necessary to get the company to resolve my problem, but I don't need to be agitated and I don't need to invent facts or expectations about their customer service agent to accomplish this.

I am expecting my husband to help clean up the kitchen. If he doesn't, I would feel angry, resentful, and taken for granted. But then I would be agitated and in pain, and all because I created this expectation. Therefore, my higher interest demands that I remove it. I can still do whatever I judge is necessary to resolve or change the situation, but to do this I don't need to be agitated or make up facts or expectations about my husband or anyone else.

Of course, on a given call, the customer service agent may turn out to be and do just what you were expecting, as may your husband after a given meal. But no one gets lucky every time, and eventually some one or other expectation you create and harbor will explode in your psyche. Removing such expectations before this happens is like buying auto insurance or getting a tetanus shot or having safe sex: by simple foresight and prevention, you immunize yourself against trouble that may be unlikely, but really bad if it happens.

Activate your no-expectation imagination.

Once you are fully aware of the existence and danger of a given expectation, it is relatively easy to remove it. It requires nothing more than noting that you have the option of expecting nothing (instead of something) of people and situations, and *imagining yourself exercising it*. Below are examples using some of the sample expectations from the beginning of the chapter. Once you activate your imagination in this way, see how many people and situations you can apply it to that you would normally and habitually form expectations about.

Situation	Situation + Imagination
I am expecting not to be unfairly fired from my job.	It is possible to have my job but not expect that for certain I'll never be unfairly fired.
I am expecting that other people will understand me and my motives.	It is possible to interact with others without expecting with absolute certainty that they will understand me or my motives.
I am expecting that I will never become disillusioned with my mentor or guru.	It's possible to have & benefit from a mentor or guru, but not expect that for sure I'll never become disillusioned with him.
I'm expecting that everyone I love will still be alive when I wake up tomorrow.	It is possible to live without expecting that for certain, everyone I love will still be alive when I wake up tomorrow.

C. Exercises for Eliminating Expectations

The following exercises combine the principles discussed above and address both expectations that have not yet caused agitation and those that have.

Exercise for exposing and removing "unexploded" expectations
- Pick a person/situation; observe the thoughts you have about him/her/it.
- Take each thought and ask yourself: Is this actually an expectation?
- See if you can translate the thought into "expectation format."
- Identify all the lower-nature agitations the expectation could cause.
  - "If I expect X and it doesn't happen, I will feel bitter and resentful."
  - "If I expect Y and it doesn't happen, I will feel jealous and possessive."
  - "If I expect Z and it doesn't happen, I will feel irritated and critical."
- Note if such reactions did happen, they would be your responsibility.
  - They would be caused by you—the "expecter."
  - They would not be caused by another person/situation—the "expectee."
- Note that such reactions would not serve your higher interest.
  - Consider the (self-inflicted) harm they would cause you.
  - Consider the harm they could cause others.
- *Then imagine it is possible to let go of the expectation/ replace it with nothing.*
  - "I can talk to X without expecting anything from her."
  - "I can work with Y without expecting anything from him."
  - "I can attend Z without expecting anything from it."
- Note the effect of this imagining on how you feel:
  - Lighter—expectations are a weighty burden to lug around.
  - Less cluttered—expectations take up space in the psyche.
  - Calmer—expectations are stressful to harbor.
  - More energized—expectations require energy to create and maintain.
  - Freer—expectations are bondage, restricting thought, feeling, & action.

Exercise for dealing with exploded expectations
- Begin by affirming the PLS principles about agitation:
  - "My agitation is caused by my own lower nature."
  - "It is not caused by any person or outer situation."
  - "It is my problem and my responsibility to solve."
  - Adopting this attitude focuses your attention on problem-solving.
- Then ask yourself, "Was an expectation behind this agitation?"
  - Review your attitude toward the person/situation before agitation began.
  - See if your thoughts & feelings can translate into "expectation format."
- If yes, note how it was the direct and sole cause of the agitation.
  - "I created and harbored an expectation about X."
  - "The expectation was in effect a land mine lying in my psyche."

- ○ "X 'stepped on' and exploded it by not fulfilling my expectation."
- ○ "The result was the lower-nature agitation/reaction I now suffer."
- Then use your imagination to relive the incident without the expectation.
  - ○ Imagine catching the expectation before the incident and removing it.
  - ○ Imagine encountering the person/ situation without the expectation.
  - ○ Imagine how differently you would feel and react.
  - ○ Use the results of this imagining for similar future situations.

D. The "Expect Nothing" Principle in Action

Let us again observe our friend Robin, this time as she applies the "expect nothing" principles to the situation with her son. We begin as usual at the point where she contemplates the "F" on his report card. We observe frustration, anger, disappointment, and disbelief roiling her psyche.

> I'm flabbergasted! An F?! I would never in a million years have thought my son would make an F. No child blessed with as many educational advantages as I've given him should ever make below a B. ... I am so mad I can't see straight, all because of him. And disappointed, too. I expected so much better from him.

With this last thought, Robin realizes, "Oops, I have an expectation problem." So she pulls out the checklist she has made for herself and reads through it:

My "Expect Nothing" Checklist

- Am I expecting something? Am I...
  - ○ Counting on, relying on, depending on something to happen?
  - ○ Analyzing beliefs/lower reactions to see if they are expectations?
  - ○ Can I translate any thoughts/feelings to "I was expecting that...?
- Do I remember: expectations are land mines I lay in my own psyche?
  - ○ Eventually someone/something will "step on one"/explode it.
  - ○ Every explosion releases toxic agitation and is my own fault.
- Are my expectations harming other people? Am I...
  - ○ Radiating demands, then punishment for not fulfilling them?
  - ○ "Energy-attacking" others through disapproval/condemnation?
- Do I remember that I can expect nothing from *any* person/situation?

The review orients Robin to the problem and calms her mind, and she notes:

> Yes, I was hugely expecting something—counting on it, depending on it—and even worse, I didn't even realize it. So, oblivious me laid a big fat land mine in my psyche, and that is right where it blew up. It's difficult to admit it, but the fact is it's totally my own fault; I'm the one who put it there and caused myself all this turmoil.

This analysis clarifies the problem, and Robin realizes she can solve it using an imaginative exercise. We observe her thoughts:

> My son made an F and may make another one at some point. I cannot depend on this not happening, but I foolishly invented the idea that such a thing was possible. I need to remove this expectation pronto. … [Reviews how the expectation was born and how unconscious it was. Imagines herself without it. Starts to feel freer and lighter.] … Wow, I didn't realize what a weight this was. … [Imagines viewing the report card without any expectations—or explosions.] … OK, I get it! This is not that hard an adjustment. Later I'll meditate more and search for other hidden expectations about my son. I do *not* want to cause myself any more needless grief.

E. Summary

- Expectations are ideas/beliefs that we create about people/situations.
- Expectations are dangerous or not depending on how we define them:
  - No danger: "Things likely to happen—but they might not."
  - Danger: "Things I can rely on, count on, depend on happening."
- Every dangerous expectation is a psychological land mine.
  - We create these land mines and lay them in our own psyche.
  - Eventually some person/situation will "step on" one & explode it.
- Exploding expectations harm ourselves.
  - The explosion releases toxic lower-nature agitation.
  - The agitation is our own fault and against our higher interest.
- Expectations harm other people.
  - We make illegal demands of them.
  - We punish them for not fulfilling these demands.
  - Our disapproval and condemnation is an unfair "energy-attack."
  - All such attacks are an egregious violation of "soul courtesy."
- The solution to the expectation problem lies in a single sentence:
  - *Expect nothing from any person, event, or circumstance.*
  - To apply this successfully, we must be aware of our expectations.

- Recognize the different types of expectations:
  - Some are explicit and easy to see.
  - Some are implicit that we never think about.
  - Some are hidden/disguised as ideals, beliefs, and conduct codes.
- Study lower-nature reactions to see if they reveal expectations.
  - Hidden expectations often manifest only through agitation.
  - Ask: "Is an expectation behind this thought or feeling?"
  - Try to translate to expectation format: "I was expecting that…"
- Seek expectations lurking in ordinary, mundane situations.
- Once you find expectations, recall the "land mine" scenario.
  - Expectations appear benign while lying quietly in your psyche.
  - They *will* cause pain and suffering if they explode.
  - Prevent this by removing such expectations before this happens.
- Activate your "no expectation" imagination.
  - It is possible to expect nothing of people and situations.
  - Imagine yourself exercising this option.

6

REJECTING UNNECESSARY SERIOUSNESS

A. The Problem

We routinely use the word *serious* to describe two different phenomena. For example, if we say that a woman is "serious about her job," we might mean that she has an earnest, focused, responsible attitude that results in her being a hard worker and taking care to do the job right and well. But we might also mean that whenever she is thinking about or doing her job, she always *feels* and radiates a heavy, anxious humorlessness.

Clearly, this first type of mental and "actional" seriousness is essential and desirable: to succeed in any important undertaking, we must think seriously about the ideas involved and act seriously to apply them. But the second type of feeling seriousness—the kind we mean when we say someone "takes things too seriously"—is both unnecessary and undesirable.

In most of us, the desirable and undesirable versions of seriousness occur together. Whenever the woman above thinks seriously about her job, it is quite likely that she simultaneously feels serious and humorless. This tendency to feel serious while we think and act extends into practically every area of our lives: relationships, school, work, child-rearing, finances, errands, conversations, chores, analyses, purchases.

Further, like a barnacle attached to a ship, feeling serious is also regularly attached to other feelings. Virtually all lower-nature reactions demonstrate this coupling:

We feel irritated—and it's serious.	We feel afraid—and it's serious.
We feel anxious—and it's serious.	We feel jealous—and it's serious.
We feel self-pity—and it's serious.	We feel angry—and it's serious.

It is impossible to overstate the extent to which this phenomenon is woven into the fabric of human life. For many people, feeling serious is a permanent background presence in their psyche.

Now when two things repeatedly arise or occur together—like thoughts of being wronged and feelings of revenge, or mental images of sex and sexual desire—we often assume that it is their nature to be forever linked. So it is with the two types of seriousness: they occur together, so they *seem* inseparable, and naturally so. We observe, for example, "I'm thinking seriously about a conflict with my girlfriend, so of course I *feel* serious about it, too—as I always do." Most of us never question this "seeming"; we just accept it and live with it. But as with so many things, what *seems* is not what *is*: feeling serious does *not* in fact have to accompany thinking and acting seriously.

And why does the PLS consider it crucial to separate them? Simply because feeling-serious is just another lower-nature quality and type of agitation, no different from hatred or vanity or anger or countless others. It is not part of our higher nature; it has no higher purpose; it does not enhance or elevate or enable us in any way. On the contrary, like all lower-nature qualities, "taking things seriously" in the wrong way mars our life:

- It is a literal psychic weight that we drag around, burdening not only ourselves but others we inadvertently radiate it to.
- It makes it seem like "something is wrong"—when really *it itself is what is wrong!*
- It makes it seem like "something seriously matters"—when really that "something" may matter very little (if at all).
- It distorts our perspective and judgment about people, events, and circumstances we encounter.
- It actually interferes with our doing successfully or well any activity we are "serious" about.
- It makes it harder than necessary to free ourselves from lower reactions like fear or irritation that it is attached to.
- And, besides all this, *it is just plain not fun*: who enjoys feeling heavy and humorless and serious all the time, or any of the time?

Therefore, it is vital to our higher interest that we amputate this "feeling-serious" component from our thoughts and actions.

Note that doing this does not diminish by one iota our motivation, drive, skill, judgment, ability to focus, attention to detail, or any other essential part of any task or undertaking. A surgeon who liberates herself from undesirable seriousness does not become less skilled or focused or careful when performing an operation. A student similarly freed does not concentrate less well or desire a lesser grade when studying for an exam. Thus we can perform even the most serious matters perfectly well while not *feeling* serious about them—discussing a difficult relationship conflict, navigating through a serious illness, wrestling with a troublesome psychological pattern. In fact, we can do all these serious activities better when we do not inflict on ourselves the added burden of feeling serious about them.

B. The Solution

Happily, feeling-serious is one of the easier PLS problems to address, because it is not really built in to the thoughts, feelings, and actions it is attached to—it is just a psychic hitchhiker, as it were. This is not, however, to minimize it as a source of bondage. In my experience, wrong seriousness is a far more significant affliction than most people realize; for some, it even turns out to be their biggest "non-dispassion" problem.

The technique for eliminating this problem consists of the six principles below, plus the exercises in the following section. Using these will both remove the unnecessary seriousness and make it easier to remove all the other lower-nature reactions it is attached to.

Develop an awareness of feeling-serious.

Feeling-serious is so pervasive and habitual, and it occurs so automatically, that most people are quite unconscious of the degree to which they feel serious, and how often. So the first step in the technique is three-fold:

- Search your consciousness for the presence of feeling-serious.
- Develop a hyper-vigilance for recognizing when it arises.
- In every situation, ask yourself, "Am I feeling serious?"

Keep your eye on lower-nature reactions.

As we noted earlier, feeling-serious nearly always accompanies other lower-nature reactions. Study this phenomenon attentively so that you can quickly identify and isolate the feeling-serious component of every agitation you experience. This will enable you to address the seriousness as a separate issue from whatever it is attached to—a critical skill, because *feeling serious needlessly prolongs all other reactions.* If, for example, you feel irritated, it is much easier to silence it if you do not feel serious about it. Sometimes, you cannot silence it at all unless you first eliminate the feeling-serious. And often when you do this, you discover that feeling-serious was actually a bigger problem than the agitation it was attached to.

Watch for the disguised forms of feeling-serious.
Earlier we noted two effects produced by feeling-serious that at first glance seem unrelated to it: the feelings that "something is wrong" and "something matters." Watch attentively for these, for they are just outward disguises assumed by feeling-serious. Once you unmask them, it is easy to see how nothing is actually wrong (except feeling-serious itself), and that what seems so important probably matters little, if at all.

Recall the dispassion choice and apply it to seriousness.
In every situation, you have two choices: (1) have the situation or (2) have the situation and feel serious about it. Here is how the choices look in table form, using some of our familiar examples from Chapter 3:

Choice #1—Situation	Choice #2—Situation + Seriousness
Have a flat tire	Have a flat tire, plus feel serious
Flight is canceled	Flight is canceled, plus feel serious
Guilt-tripped by mother	Guilt-tripped by mother, plus feel serious
Fired from job	Fired from job, plus feel serious
Hit every red light	Hit every red light, plus feel serious

Choice #2 is always against your higher interest, because feeling-serious is a lower-nature energy. Choice #1—situation minus seriousness—always furthers your higher interest, plus it is your birthright: *you do not have to feel serious about any situation whatsoever,* even those requiring serious thought and action.

Activate your "non-seriousness" imagination.
Once you remember that you always have the option not to feel serious, then direct your imagination to this goal. Here are examples from recent consultations I have had with PLS users:

Situation	Situation + Imagination
I need to talk to my partner about a conflict.	It is possible to talk seriously with him/her without feeling serious.
I have an important job interview.	It is possible to have the interview without feeling serious about it.
I am planning a dinner party.	It is possible to have the party without feeling serious about it.
I am teaching a drawing class.	It is possible to teach the class and not feel serious about how it goes.
My skin is ageing.	It is possible for my skin to age without my feeling serious about it.
My parents don't understand me.	It is possible for my parents not to understand me without my feeling serious about it.

Make a game of seeing just how many things that you habitually take seriously can be struck off your list. Push the non-seriousness into as many unexpected areas as possible. The situations and agitations that you can add to your "this-is-not-serious" list are limited only by your imagination.

Build a reservoir of non-seriousness.

Remember that exercising your imagination in advance of situations and activities you expect to feel serious about produces the maximum effect. Sustained, directed imagination actually generates a protective "reservoir" of non-serious energy which neutralizes any feeling-serious energy that should arise. Further, when you do this enough times, you create a new "non-serious habit," which eventually displaces your old "serious" habit.

Here is an example from my own experience. As I am writing this chapter, I am pestered by the following thoughts: "This is not working, and I'll never get it right." "My whole conception of how to structure the sections is wrong." "I've tried so many ways of doing this, but none of them work." All these thoughts naturally tend to have feeling-serious attached to them. Yet as each thought arises, it runs into the habit of non-seriousness and the reservoir of non-serious energy I have generated over many years. As a result, I maintain a feeling of lightness and good humor. I don't feel serious, even while thinking and writing as seriously as I can. If I don't get it right the first time, it's not serious. If it takes a hundred times, that's not serious either. Even if at some point I have to abandon everything and start over, still not serious. So, no matter what the writing scenario, the "non-serious" reservoir and habit successfully preempt feeling-serious.

C. Exercises for Eliminating Seriousness

The following exercises combine all the principles discussed above and address the two common instances of seriousness.

Seriousness attached to other reactions
- Pick a troublesome reaction and visualize it clearly.
- Observe that when this reaction arises, you simultaneously feel serious about it.
- Feel the reaction and seriousness together, as you normally experience them.
- Then recall that *the reaction and the seriousness are two different things*.
- Contemplate how this is so & separate the two things in your consciousness.
- Then imagine it's possible to have the reaction but not feel serious about it.
  - "I can feel afraid without feeling serious about it."
  - "I can feel worried without feeling serious about it."
  - "I can feel self-pity without feeling serious about it."
- Note the results of this imagining.
  - The reaction is less menacing/painful when you stop feeling serious about it.
  - Not taking it seriously lessens its power over you and helps you release it.

Seriousness in your general disposition
- Inventory your psyche for the presence of the three types of seriousness:
  - Feeling of general seriousness
  - Feeling that something is wrong
  - Feeling that something matters
- Search every area you can think of—relationships, job, family, children, etc.
- Then subject each to a meditation with the following themes:
  - Is it really necessary to feel serious about a given situation?
  - Is it really necessary to feel that something is wrong with a given situation?
  - Is it really necessary for a given situation to matter so much, or at all?
- Consider every situation you feel serious about.
  - Is the matter really, honestly as serious as you are feeling?
  - Is it possible that it is far less serious, or not serious at all?
  - Apply the full scope of your imagination to these possibilities.
- Consider every situation you feel there is something wrong about.
  - Is anything really wrong?
  - Is it possible that nothing is really wrong at all?
  - Apply the full scope of your imagination to these possibilities.

- Consider every situation that you feel "seriously matters."
  - Does it really, honestly matter so much?
  - Is it possible that it does not really matter at all, or at least very little?
  - Apply the full scope of your imagination to these possibilities.

D. Non-Seriousness in Action

Let us again observe our friend Robin, this time as she applies the non-serious principles to the situation with her son. When she contemplates the "F" on his report card, we see a surge of instinctive agitation in her psyche: frustration, anger, disappointment, disbelief, etc. She remembers that all such reactions are prime candidates to have feeling-serious attached to them, so she consults a checklist she has made for herself:

> **My "Non-Seriousness" Checklist**
>
> - Am I feeling serious?
>   - Did it arise independently or attached to a lower-nature reaction?
>   - Is it masquerading as "something is wrong" or "something matters"?
> - Do I remember that feeling-serious is a lower agitation?
>   - It does not enhance, elevate, empower, or enable me in any way.
>   - It prevents me from freeing myself from reactions it is attached to.
>   - It actually interferes with dealing with situations—and it's not fun!
> - Do I remember that it is not necessary to feel serious?
>   - In any situation, I can think & act seriously without feeling serious.
>   - Doing so ensures that I retain full access to my best self & qualities.
> - Doing so lets me address situations effectively, humorously, & lightly.

This review orients Robin to the problem and calms her mind, and she notes:

> Yes, feeling-serious is attached to all the lower energies roiling my psyche. And yes, it does feel like something is terribly wrong and of great importance—but that doesn't mean it's true. And even if it were, feeling serious is not going to help me address the situation; only serious thought and action can do that. Plus, I hate feeling serious! And I certainly don't want to feel it now on top of dealing with my son and his F.

With this attitude in place, Robin decides to sit down and run through a quick non-serious exercise. We observe her thoughts:

My feeling of seriousness is separate from my frustration, anger, and disappointment. ... I don't have to feel serious about them. ... [Starts imagining this. The tension in her psyche immediately begins subsiding. She sighs with relief.] ... OK, I don't need to be agitated or feel serious about this F. Nothing is wrong that can't be fixed. It's not the end of the world. The problem is solvable.

She then begins imagining how to deal non-seriously with the situation.

- I can talk to my son about his grade—but without feeling serious.
- I can have a conference with his teacher—but without feeling serious.
- I can get him a tutor—but without feeling serious.
- I can try to make him study more—but without feeling serious.
- I can restrict his freedom if necessary—but without feeling serious.

She affirms that each of these actions addresses the situation (the "F"), yet leaves her without a problem (feeling-serious, frustration, anger, and disappointment). And to prevent future unnecessary seriousness in this matter, she asserts to herself:

> It is possible that none of these actions will work, and my son will fail his class and have to retake it. But if he does, he can fail without my feeling serious, and he can retake it without my feeling serious. Whatever happens, I can do my best to help him, but while not feeling serious. And if I do this, I'll be helping him, too, as he'll enjoy being around me and my best self, and I won't be burdening him with a radiation of heavy, humorless seriousness that helps neither of us.

Here is another example of non-seriousness applied to life, as described by a PLS user in a recent consultation:

> Recently I've been able to extend my application of the non-serious principle from external situations ("I have a flat tire, and it's not serious") to emotional reactions that don't always have clear external triggers, like anger or sadness or the threat of depression, or even wrong seriousness itself.
>
> All my life, I've regarded emotional reactions as very, very serious. Now I'm able to have the attitude, "I'm having a strong emotional reaction—and even this is not serious." Naturally, I can't always remember this principle, but when I forget, that's not serious either. But when I've remembered to try it, the shift in my attitude is so freeing that the repeated practice convinces me that I'm going in the right direction.

My old view was that when I felt angry, it was very serious and I should not feel that way, because I falsely believed that being spiritual meant I had to rid myself of all emotions. My new view is that when I'm angry, it's not serious. It's a normal human reaction, and I don't have to do anything about it in the way I thought I did before: ask for forgiveness, ask for help out of neediness or desperation, confront anybody, defend myself, etc. This lets me absorb the anger, so to speak, rather than act on it, holding it gently and lightly while it runs its course —simple but not easy—all the while reminding myself that even strong emotional reactions are "normal" and not serious. And if I forget myself and act on the anger—that's not serious either! This is a whole new way of accepting myself by accepting the fact that I do have emotions, and all of them are not serious! It's amazing that such a simple shift in attitude could produce such a huge beneficent effect.

E. Summary

- Thinking seriously & acting seriously are crucial to any undertaking.
- Feeling-serious contributes nothing useful to any undertaking.
- Feeling-serious is a "stand-alone" lower-nature agitation.
- Feeling-serious is also attached to most other lower-nature agitations.
- Feeling-serious mars our life:
  - Burdens us, and others we radiate it to, with its psychic weight.
  - Makes it seem like "something is wrong," when *it* is what's wrong.
  - Makes it harder to free ourselves from agitation it is attached to.
  - Distorts our perspective and judgment about people and situations.
  - Interferes with our dealing successfully with people and situations.
  - Robs us of fun, lightness, humor, and the joy of living.
- Therefore, it is in our higher interest to subtract feeling-serious.
- We can still think and act seriously even when we do not feel serious.
- In every situation we have two choices:
  - Choice 1—We can have the situation.
  - Choice 2—We can have the situation and feel serious about it.
- Choice 1 requires us to imagine the possibility of not feeling serious.
- Sustained "non-serious" imagining creates two desirable effects:
  - A reservoir of non-serious energy that absorbs feeling-serious.
  - A new "non-serious" habit that displaces the old "serious" one.

7

LEARNING & EXPERIMENTATION

A. Introduction

Anyone who masters a task or develops a skill always does so through a graded learning process. All such processes are governed by the same few basic principles and have the same clearly identifiable stages between rank beginner and accomplished master. Whether the skill is making bread, playing the violin, building a house, or performing brain surgery, the science of how learning happens is the same.

Using the Personal Liberation System is no exception to this rule. Here is a partial list of PLS techniques we have introduced so far:

- Ask the interest question: "Is a proposed action in my higher interest?"
- Discard the old view of problems (they are caused by outer situations).
- Adopt the new view of problems (they are caused by inner agitation).
- Remember the difference between situations and problems.
- Remember the two choices that exist in every situation.
- Use the imagination to reject the "situation + agitation" choice.
- Accept the facts without wishing or hoping they were different.
- Expect nothing from any person, event, or circumstance.
- Amputate feeling-serious from thinking and acting.

Succeeding chapters will present four more dispassion techniques, as well as numerous meditation ones. All these techniques are skills we have to acquire through the standard learning process. Therefore, in this chapter we will pause our presentation of techniques to study the science involved in learning them—what the stages of the process are, why each is necessary, what to expect in them, and what they require of us. Knowing these things will not only help us learn faster, but also eliminate unnecessary reactions to the process itself as it is happening.

There is another reason for this study as well. As we shall see, experimentation is the most crucial component of learning, and thus a free, experimental spirit is an essential quality for mastering each PLS technique. Yet cultivating and applying such a spirit does something more: it is actually a technique of liberation in its own right. It transforms any life into a fascinating laboratory in which each situation or problem, however difficult or intractable, is a welcome opportunity to experiment, learn, and master. Many PLS users find that this one idea alone —of free and imaginative experimentation—revolutionizes their outlook on life and gives them a new freedom and joy.

We will divide our study into three sections: the process of learning, the practical implications of the learning principles, and the enemies of learning.

B. The Process of Learning

Perhaps the best way to illustrate how all learning happens is to study an example of a blind woman who seeks to traverse an unfamiliar corridor. She cannot see, but she has a "white cane" that she can swing before her. Using it, she must figure out how to get from the corridor's entrance to its exit. The diagrams below record her successive attempts to learn this task.

In the initial attempt, it takes the woman many strikes of her cane and many changes of direction to reach the exit. She makes nearly every "mistake" it is possible to make, hitting six walls and seven objects. Yet all these experiences leave her with a rough internal "map" of the corridor.

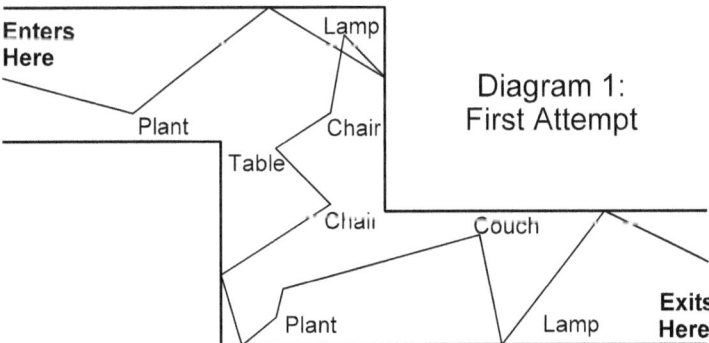

Diagram 1: First Attempt

The second try goes much more smoothly. The woman strikes only the table (she is still unclear about its size and location) and a lamp (she did not encounter it the first time). When she reaches the exit at the end of the second try, she knows enough to say, "Ah-ha! Now I 'see'."

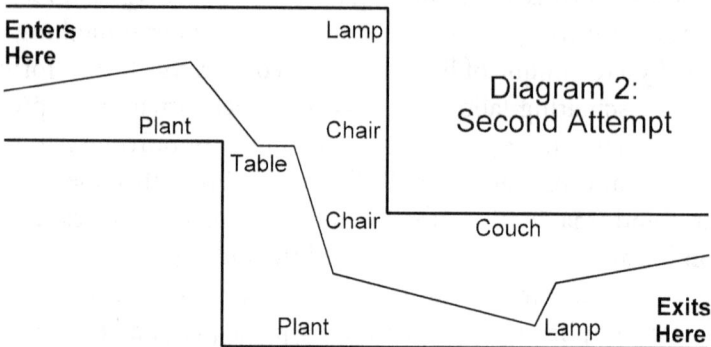

By the third attempt, the woman has no problems; she has learned the route based on her previous experiences and can traverse it at will. If she wants to "know" the whole corridor—height of the ceiling, items on the walls, chairs around the table, etc.—she can "map" it by more cane swings. Then she will thoroughly know and have mastered the corridor.

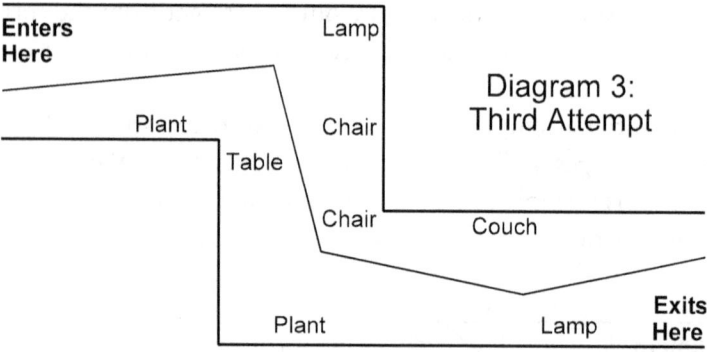

This simple example contains all the principles, processes, and stages of learning that will apply to every PLS technique.

- We begin "blind" and learn to "see" through experience.
- We have a "dispassion cane," "non-seriousness cane," "meditation cane," etc., to "swing" to acquire the needed experiences.
- We learn as our experiences multiply and we study their lessons.
- We have an "ah-ha!" moment of realization when we have accumulated enough experiences.
- We master a technique when we practice enough times what we realized in the "ah-ha!" moment.

Now let us state these ideas formally as a series of principles of learning, with comments on each principle.

All learning begins with experimentation.
The blind woman cannot begin to "learn" the corridor until she starts swinging the cane. Every swing of the cane is an experiment. The same is true of all PLS learning—every attempt at dispassion, meditation, etc., is an experiment of some sort.

All experiments produce experiences, or "experience-units."
An experience-unit is simply a cause-effect sequence: A swing of the white cane (action) either does or does not strike something (effect). A finger stuck into a fire (action) gets burned (effect). The elimination of an expectation (action) produces a lack of agitation (effect). These experience-units constitute raw "data" available for us to analyze: we act, observe what happens, and adjust our next action accordingly.

Experience-units are of two basic types: positive and negative.
"Positive" units show us how *to* do a thing (what works); "negative" units show us how *not* to do a thing (what does not work). For our blind woman, swinging her cane and striking nothing generates a positive unit: it shows that the way ahead is clear and she *can* go forward in that direction. Conversely, when her swinging cane strikes something, it creates a negative unit: it indicates that an obstruction is ahead, and she *cannot* go forward by that route. Note that "positive" and "negative" do not mean "good" and "bad," but simply denote two opposite types of data, both necessary.

Experience-units accumulate, producing "experience-piles."
All the positive and negative experience-units we generate pass into our psyche and cluster together into "experience-piles." These piles constitute our accumulated experience in a given area of life. We might picture them as in the diagram below, then note two important facts about them:

Relationship Pile	Meditation Pile	Violin Pile	Corridor Pile
⊕⊖	⊕⊖⊕	⊖⊖⊕	⊖
⊖⊕⊖⊖⊖⊕	⊖⊕⊕⊖⊖⊕	⊕⊖⊖⊕	⊖⊖⊕⊖
⊕⊖⊕⊖⊖	⊖⊖⊕⊖⊖	⊖⊖⊕⊖⊖⊕	⊕⊕⊖⊖
⊖⊖⊖	⊖⊖⊖⊕	⊖⊖⊕⊖⊕⊖	⊖⊖⊕

First, a fully-formed, "mature" experience-pile typically contains a larger number of negative units than positive ones. This mix mirrors life, since for most skills or tasks, there are far more "ways that don't work" than "ways that do work."

Second, as the positive and negative results of experimentation accumulate in a given experience-pile, they gradually form a mosaic "picture" of a situation or task. For the blind woman, this picture is a "corridor map" in her mind's eye. This picture depends for its existence on both types of experiment outcomes: no positive *and* negative, no map. We need both types to learn, and experience-piles with the greatest number of both "what works" and "what doesn't work" inevitably make the most accurate and useful maps.

When an experience-pile reaches a critical size, an "ah-ha!" moment of realization or knowing occurs.

A perfect example of this process is learning to ride a bicycle. Most of us probably spent the early stages of the learning process awkwardly generating experience-units: yanking the handle bars from side to side trying to keep our balance, thrusting our feet out to keep from falling, trying to pedal and steer at the same time, and even crashing a few times. But eventually our accumulated experiences reached the critical mass, and then suddenly, everything fell into place, and we realized how to ride—our "ah-ha!" moment.

The same process will inevitably occur in learning a PLS skill, say, for example, practicing dispassion. Some person or situation will provoke us. Our first attempt to react calmly will fail, and we will find ourselves agitated. In the midst of the turbulence, we will eventually remember to search for expectations and wishful thinking, and we will become dimly aware of how unnecessarily serious we are feeling. Then we will begin imagining and experimenting how to remove the expectations and accept the facts and not feel serious. After some repetitions of this cycle, our accumulations will reach a sufficient size, and suddenly, receiving a familiar provocation, we will find ourselves unagitated and not serious, and we will realize how to do it and how it can be done in other, similar circumstances.

Continued additions to the experience-pile lead to mastery.

The "ah-ha!" moment does not mark the end of the learning process; it is simply the point where we realize how something works. At this stage, the technique or method we now understand still requires conscious effort and concentrated attention. In our bicycle example, at the moment when we realized how to ride, and for some time afterwards, we still had to pay close attention to coordinate all the movements and balancing. Only after more hours of riding did the skill become automatic and effortless, so that we became a master of cycling. The same will be true in our quest to master every PLS technique.

Thus it is vital not to confuse knowing and understanding with mastery. Much work remains to be done after the moment of realization. Mastery is attained only through practice—many repetitions based on acquired knowing. Note that these repetitions increase not only the size, but also the density of the experience-pile, creating a solid, reliable foundation on which to stand. This ultimately enables us to wield our skill or ability with poise and balance in all circumstances.

The chart below illustrates the three major stages in every learning process:

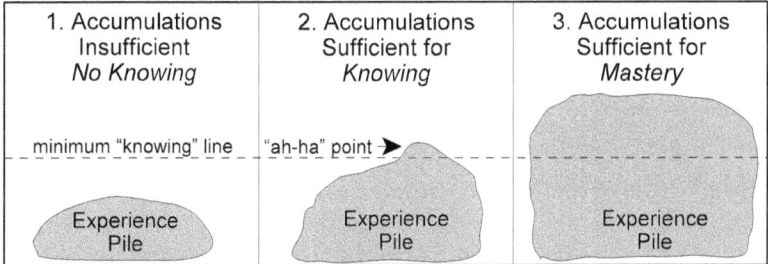

Summary of the Learning Principles
- Learning is a chain of activities fueled by experimentation: experiment > experience > accumulations > knowing > mastery
- The learning process has two divisions:
  - Not-yet-knowing demands more experimentation
  - Not-yet-a-master demands more practice.

C. Implications of the Principles of Learning

Now let us consider what these learning principles imply for users of the PLS. Most of these implications are obvious; none will surprise.

To learn, we must act.
Newton's first Law of Motion (often called the Law of Inertia) states:

A body at rest tends to remain at rest, and a body in motion tends to remain in motion in the same direction, *unless acted upon by an external force.*

This same law works equally within our psyche in the matter of learning. We begin in an inert, static state of not knowing, which will continue indefinitely until we act. Only action—swinging our experiment "cane"—can start and propel the learning chain. A passage in *The Mahatma Letters* perhaps best encapsulates this idea: "We have but one word for all aspirants—TRY." It is no more complicated than that: trying is the fuel that propels our movement along the learning chain, disrupting the status quo and opening doors we may never have known existed.

Initial accumulations are necessarily collected unknowingly, in the dark.
Prior to experimenting, we cannot know or be able, so all learning must begin from blindness and inability. Our beginning actions are often difficult, awkward, inept, unsuccessful. While trying them, we often feel frustrated, uncomfortable, self-doubting, dispirited, hopeless. Such feelings are misleading—they do not indicate that something is wrong, and they are not serious. Furthermore, paying attention to them actually retards the learning process. As long as we continue to act, even if blindly, our actions produce effects which accumulate, guiding us toward eventual knowing.

The speed of learning depends on the amount of experimentation.
An experiment of meditating twice a day for thirty minutes generates three times more experience-units than one of meditating once a day for twenty minutes. Over time, this obviously produces a substantial difference in the size of our experience-pile, and thus our skill. But the difference does not end there, because the more we know, the faster we can learn. So as our meditation skill increases, the pace of our learning accelerates. The ideal PLS user will thus seize every opportunity to apply each PLS technique. Rapid learning is possible through non-stop experimentation.

There is no such thing as a mistake or failure.
Experience-piles contain positive units and negative units, but no "mistake units." The blind woman never thinks, "My cane hit an object; I have made a terrible mistake!" Instead, she is grateful to know, "Here is a wall or a table or a chair; I now know to try elsewhere." To her, the concept of "cane-swing mistake" would be nonsensical.

Negative experience-units—the ones we often thoughtlessly label "mistakes" —are just as important and necessary as positive ones. They direct the search for truth and mastery by showing us, "This thing and everything like it are *not* it." Thomas Edison best expressed this scientific attitude in a famous statement:

> If I find 10,000 ways something won't work, I haven't failed. I am not discouraged, because every wrong attempt discarded is one more step forward.

The true scientist wins and rejoices whenever he is experimenting. He does not care whether the outcome is "works" or "doesn't work," because after every experiment, he knows more than before. As PLS users we must cultivate this same scientific attitude, taking special care to (1) reject the notion that we have done anything "wrong" when an experiment generates a negative experience-unit; (2) not care how many swings of our "PLS-techniques cane" are necessary to produce an accurate map; and (3) always continue the experiments, confident that each result directs us inexorably toward knowing and mastery.

No experience ever is or could be wasted or purposeless.

All experiences enter our psyche-container and, once inside, reside there permanently. Each experience without exception helps to build the experience-pile and therefore contributes to learning—even if it seems otherwise.

D. Enemies of Learning

No matter how well we understand the learning principles above, when we start applying them we are likely to encounter obstacles. For the unprepared, these obstacles can quickly sabotage even the best-intentioned learning project, usually by preventing the crucial first step —experimentation. Fortunately, we can sidestep these obstacles fairly easily if we know what they are and plan a response to them; forewarned is forearmed. Here are the most common.

We are paralyzed by the illusory concept of "mistake."

As we have seen, there is no such thing as a mistake. But realizing this fact mentally usually does not immediately free us from the instinctive, deep-seated fear of making one. This fear is a feeling of dread and foreboding that if we do not confine ourselves to a narrow band of "authority-approved" or "society-approved" activities, but instead experiment freely as our inner light directs us, we will surely make terrible errors and call down upon our head guilt, shame, humiliation, condemnation, rejection, and ostracism. Ouch!

Really the only way to deal with this wildly irrational fear is to acknowledge it and experiment anyway. Most of the time we will find that the moment the experiment begins, the fear is disproved and loses its power; nothing silences static fear more effectively than dynamic experimentation. And remember: if we make a "mistake" or "fail," nothing is wrong and it's not serious—ever.

We lack a developed "experiment-imagination."

The long reign of "mistake-fear" and non-experimentation has left most people with little, if any, developed skill at imagining experiment opportunities and picturing how to take advantage of them. For the PLS user, removing this limitation requires two major adjustments.

First, we must adopt the view that everything we do, at every moment, already *is* an experiment. Conversing with a friend, visiting a web site, exploring a new relationship, reading this book—all these are experiments in which we act and experience the results. Shifting to this perspective naturally awakens our mind to ways that we might creatively use each element in our life-laboratory to apply and practice the PLS techniques.

Second, when we encounter a difficulty or impasse, we must picture how we might experiment our way to a resolution. This means stretching our imagination beyond the usual, obvious options. For example, suppose a married couple with relationship problems cannot decide whether to divorce. As PLS users, they hit upon the idea to rent an apartment and take turns living alone in it. This experience furnishes them with direct, non-speculative answers to certain crucial questions: Do I like being apart? Do I feel better now, or worse? Am I afraid? Am I relieved? Is this what I want? Does it feel right? Of course, this imaginative experiment alone may not solve their problem, but the experience they gain from it is certain to contribute significantly to the process.

We try to speculate our way to knowing and learning.

Most of us devote a great deal of our thought-life to speculative thinking. One aspect of such speculating can be beneficial. We think, "I wonder if this idea could lead to a better way of living" or "What might happen if I tried to accomplish this task by a different method?"

Such musings are helpful if they quickly lead to action: I am off to try this or that thing and see what happens; then I will know. Too often, however, we use speculation to try to circumvent the principles of learning. But no one's experience pile has ever been increased by speculation. At the end of speculating, what we have are speculations, not knowing or learning. The PLS user must cultivate the habit of stopping each useless speculation and replacing it with an experiment. (An entire chapter on speculation is ahead.)

Our beliefs and ideals interfere with experiments and the facts they reveal.
Belief-systems and ideals are tools for approaching the truth, and as such they can be an excellent source of hypotheses to test in experiments. But locked-in beliefs and inflexible ideals can also be a major obstacle to personal liberation (and truth). They can prejudice us against testing certain hypotheses and keep us from recognizing and accepting facts that experiments reveal. Both these results block our progress toward self-knowledge and self-mastery—the very goals that the beliefs and ideals are supposed to be helping us attain. So the less a believer and the more a scientist and truth-seeker you can be, the better the PLS will work.

We misuse books, reading them in the wrong way.
When we read books to discover methods for self-mastery, that is a valuable thing. But often when we find a promising technique, we keep reading. At that point, our reading is preventing us from acting (experimenting). In extreme cases, reading is all we do. But reading is not doing, just as looking at maps is not traveling. Thus as PLS users we must take care to treat books (like this one) as simply an instruction manual such as might accompany, say, a toaster oven or a camera: read the instructions, then set them aside and start applying the information.

We are restrained or stopped by various irrational fears.
- "If I try something new, I'm committed to it for life."

An experiment is an experiment, not a commitment. The only way you will commit to anything is if you like it, you think it is in your higher interest, and it feels right. In fact, the PLS would caution against committing to any method or approach for life, since as we grow and evolve, our learning requirements and needs change. What works and is liberating at one stage may not work—or even be imprisoning—at another.

- "I'll have to experiment with things that are too big for me to handle."

No, you can chose to experiment with any size problem you like. In fact, I always encourage new PLS users to begin by experimenting with small things and working through an entire learning cycle. The experience and confidence they gain from mastering those small challenges then lead them naturally to tackle increasingly larger ones.

- "If I experiment and try, I'll encounter obstacles and be tested."

Yes, you will. But just as resistance is necessary for strengthening muscles, so obstacles and difficulties are necessary for growth and freedom, and you will come to welcome them as interesting challenges dropped into your laboratory. As for tests, nothing is more useful (and exciting) to an inventor than opportunities to test his ideas and prototypes. Similarly, tests will quickly become your best friend in every PLS learning project, allowing you to gauge your progress, directing you how to adjust your methods, and suggesting what further experiments are necessary.

E. The Learning Principles in Action

As usual, we will end by looking in on our friend Robin as she applies the principles of this chapter to the situation with her son. As she contemplates the "F" on his report card, we see a surge of powerful agitation in her psyche: frustration, anger, disappointment, disbelief. We observe her thoughts:

> None of my children has ever made an F in school. This is new and unfamiliar territory, so I don't really know how to respond or what to do about it. But I'm obviously going to have to learn.

At the thought of learning, Robin reaches for the extensive PLS checklist [facing page] she has made for herself, and reads through it carefully.

This review steadies Robin's mind and redirects her attention toward her higher nature and best self. She pictures the ideal attitude she wants to adopt:

> I can treat this whole situation as a laboratory in which I conduct an interesting learning project. I just have to start experimenting freely and see what works and what doesn't. And I don't have to worry or feel serious about mistakes, since there aren't any; whatever I do, I'll know more after than before. Enough experimenting will eventually show me the way to master this situation and my reaction to it.

My "Learning & Experimentation" Checklist

- **Am I forgetting the only way to learn is through experimentation?**
  - Experiment > experience > accumulations > learning > mastery.
  - No experiment > no experience > no accumulation > no learning.
  - If I don't yet know/am not able, I need more experimentation.
  - If I haven't yet mastered, I need more practice (repetitions).
- **Am I overlooking opportunities for experimenting?**
  - Do I remember there is nowhere I can be that is not a laboratory?
  - Do I welcome each situation as an opportunity for experimenting?
  - Do I remember that it is legal to experiment in *every* area of life?
  - Do I remember that everything I do already *is* an experiment?
- **Am I failing to experiment continuously due to…?**
  - Fear of "mistakes" or "failure"—both illusory concepts?
  - Trying to learn through the substitute method of speculation?
  - Trying to substitute reading for doing?
  - Fear of encountering obstacles or tests—both my friends?
- **Am I forgetting that to learn, I must act?**
  - Only action can start and propel the learning chain.
  - Passivity cannot work—no outside force, no change of state.
  - "We have but one word for all aspirants—TRY."
  - Continuous trying propels me towards knowing and mastery.
  - When I try, I create new, unexpected, unforeseen possibilities.
- **Am I forgetting that all learning begins from blindness/inability?**
  - Prior to experimenting, I cannot know or be able.
  - My beginning actions are often difficult, awkward, unsuccessful.
  - I may feel frustrated, self-doubting, dispirited, hopeless.
  - Such feelings aren't serious & don't indicate something is wrong.
  - If I pay attention to them, I actually retard the learning process.
  - As long as I act, even if blindly, I produce valuable accumulations.

With this attitude in place, Robin begins imagining herself dealing with the outer situation:

- I can talk to my son about his grade—as an experiment.
- I can have a conference with his teacher—as an experiment.
- I can get him a tutor—as an experiment.
- I can try to make him study more—as an experiment.
- I can restrict his freedom—as an experiment.

While these experiments are in progress, I'm not going to fret over what the outcomes might be, or wish or hope for one outcome over another, or invent an expectation that surely one or another of them should succeed, or feel serious about them. I'm simply going to observe the results calmly and dispassionately, and use them to guide me to the next experiment, until I finally know how best to meet this situation and solve it. And I'm going to do my best to convey this spirit and method to my son, and show him how he can experiment his way out of the hole he's dug himself into.

F. Summary

- All PLS techniques are mastered through a graded learning process.
- The learning process is a chain of activities fueled by experimentation.
- Experiment => experience => accumulations => knowing => mastery
- The learning process has two divisions:
  - Not-yet-a-knower demands more experimentation.
  - Not-yet-a-master demands more practice.
- To learn, we must act.
- "We have but one word for all aspirants—TRY."
- All learning begins from blindness and inability.
- The more we experiment, the faster we learn.
- There is no such thing as a mistake.
- All experiences accumulate; no experience is wasted or purposeless.
- Anything preventing experimentation sabotages the learning process:
  - Fear of making a "mistake"
  - Lack of developed "experiment-imagination"
  - Speculation instead of experimentation
  - Attachment to beliefs and ideals
  - Misuse of books and reading
  - Confusion of experimentation with commitment
  - Fear of obstacles and tests
- A free, experimental spirit overcomes all these saboteurs.
- It is also a technique of liberation in its own right:
  - Transforms any life, however difficult, into a fascinating laboratory.
  - Frees us from imaginary limits and aligns us with our authentic self.

8

MINDING OUR OWN BUSINESS

A. The Problem

We now resume our survey of the dispassion topics with one that might at first seem odd to include. Most of us probably associate failing to mind our own business mainly with the burdensome effects it produces on the "interferee." But it is also a major source of agitation and bondage for the "interferer," and learning to leave people free is profoundly liberating.

We confront the issue of minding our own business every time we register an impulse to advise or help others in some way. This impulse can arise from a variety of motives, but whatever the source, nature's learning system decrees that there are lawful and unlawful (right and wrong) ways to render this service. The lawful way helps without coercion or interference or infringing others' free will. The unlawful one trespasses into others' affairs with uninvited energy and advice:

- We offer people unsolicited or unwanted guidance.
- We pressure and badger them to do what we suggest.
- We try to control what they think or feel or do.
- We interfere with their experiments and learning processes.
- We criticize their "mistakes" as wrong and serious and irremediable.
- We radiate frustration, intolerance, condemnation at how they live.

Interestingly, the motivation leading to such unlawful intrusions can originate in the higher as well as the lower nature. As we use the PLS or other methods to grow and expand, our higher light increasingly illumines our mind. This illumination gives us knowledge and insights that we realize could be of great use to others. Simultaneously, our awakening heart moves us to share this light to help them progress and have better, freer lives. But just because these higher energies are pure and selfless in themselves does not guarantee that when we express them to others, it will be in the lawful, non-invasive way.

Of course, our lower nature provides myriad not-so-lofty impulses to interfere as well. Instead of trying to catalogue every one of them, let us consider a shorter list (in no particular order) of common personality types. The conditioning built into these types serves as a ready conduit for the full complement of lower motives to manifest:

- **Control-freak**—for whom it is natural to dominate, dictate, coerce, manipulate, or bully others.
- **Leader**—for whom it is natural to give orders and have followers.
- **Teacher**—for whom it is natural to instruct others.
- **Engineer/problem-solver**—for whom it is natural to tell others how to perform tasks more skillfully or efficiently.
- **Zealot/Proselytizer**—for whom it is natural to regard his ideas or beliefs as THE TRUTH, and to feel duty-bound to harangue everyone about them and convert them to his camp.
- **Over-familiar family member**—for whom it is natural to consider that boundaries within the family are non-existent, and that he has a "familial right" to intervene, and that the "intervenee" would of course want him to do so and always welcome it.
- **Morality arbiter**—for whom it is natural to consider that he has a superior morality that he should impose on others.
- **General busybody**—for whom it is natural to snoop in everyone's business and collect information and gossip, with the idea of disseminating it as widely as possible.
- **Confrontationalist**—to whom it is natural to have strong private codes of conduct (often known only to himself), to see people violating those codes and no one stopping them, and so to feel an obligation and duty to step in and intervene. "I'm the only person who sees this and realizes how bad it is, so I have to do it."
- **Person obsessed with others**—for whom it is natural for his thought life to be consumed with other people, their lives, the contents of their psyche, their actions, their (supposed) needs, etc. Naturally at some point he is compelled to discharge all these thoughts onto the person who is the subject of his thought.

- **Arrogant, superior, know-it-all**—for whom it is natural to possess the attitude, "I know and you don't, so naturally and fortunately for you, and for your own good, I will tell you what you don't know and what you ought to think and do."
- **Over-protective nurturer**—for whom it is natural to mother others, hover over them, offer excessive assistance (wanted or not), and habitually rush in to "save" them.

Naturally, we could identify other personality types besides these, but even this short list suggests the nearly unlimited range of lower motives that can drive us to interfere. And when we add to the mix the higher motives discussed above, we can appreciate how many temptations we face to trespass into others' affairs.

But regardless of whether our motive for interfering is higher or lower, selfless or selfish, acting on it in the wrong way detrimentally affects both ourselves and others. When we are the interferer, we agitate ourselves in numerous ways. We waste time and energy thinking about others that we could spend on addressing our own problems. We invent the idea that others should welcome our intrusions and follow our advice, then feel frustrated, angry, impatient, critical, indignant, or hurt when they do not. We fret over the (to us) slow speed of their learning, worry about their choice of experiments, and panic about their future. All these non-dispassionate reactions inflame our lower nature and drag us down.

At the same time that we thus agitate ourselves, we inflict an equal or greater measure of suffering and trouble on other people. First, they feel an entirely justified resentment at us for our unauthorized intrusion into their affairs—just as they would if we entered their house without their permission. If the intrusions continue, they quickly lose respect for us and begin to shun our company. After all, who would want to continue a close association with someone who is a serial disrespecter of boundaries?

Second, every instance of barging into others' affairs violates their free will. This is surely the greatest of all offenses, for the success of nature's system of learning depends on the free exercise of will and the free operation of the law of cause and effect. Interfere in those in even the smallest ways in others' lives, and we thwart the system from working for them—something we have no right to do.

Third, it is simply painful to be on the receiving end of a constant stream of coercion, pressure, loaded advice, criticism, disapproval, and the like. This is nothing other than the psychological equivalent of peppering another person with physical jabs, pushes, pokes, slaps, tugs, etc. —actions that could get us arrested for battery.

Finally, intrusions and interference rob others of the undisturbed space to think quietly, weigh decisions about what actions to take, and digest the lessons those actions bring, all free of outside influence and pressure.

Note that all these actions are flagrant violations of the "soul courtesy" we discussed in Chapter 5:

> "Soul courtesy" [is] the true inner courtesy that is inherent in our higher nature and extended to all our fellow souls. It is based on the heart-knowledge that nature has endowed all humans with the freedom to live and experiment in the way they think best for them, as they struggle to find, be, and express their best self. Knowing that such a process is difficult for everyone, soul courtesy thus scrupulously avoids actions that infringe others' free will or unfairly makes their lives harder. (p. 57)

When we realize the full extent to which we can harm others as well as ourselves by failing to mind our own business, it is not an exaggeration to say that this is the most harmful and offensive of all the PLS dispassion problems. Let us analyze how to solve it.

B. The Mind-Our-Own-Business (MOOB) Principles

In the previous chapter we studied the general principles of nature's system of learning and their particular application to us personally, as individuals. We now need to consider what those principles imply about other people and our interactions with them. This will enable us to see not only what is and is not possible to others and how best to help them, but also when, how, and why to mind our own business. We can state the most important of these implications in the following axioms:

Everyone must do his own learning (build his own experience-pile).
Each person must learn for himself and by himself, since he is the only person who can generate the experience-units which enter *his* psyche and produce *his* experience-piles.

We can describe our experience pile to others, but never transfer it.
To think otherwise would be as ludicrous as to imagine that we could eat or sleep and somehow "donate" the resulting nourishment or rest to Person X, who would then be exempt from needing to eat or sleep himself. Just as X must do his own eating and sleeping, so also must he do his own learning (i.e., experimenting and accumulating).

Descriptions of knowledge are not the same as direct experience.
This is an obvious point—in theory. But in practice, we often seem to expect that if we merely *tell* Person Y of our experiences and the wisdom we gained from them, she will suddenly, magically know everything that we know and act accordingly. The reality, of course, is that our descriptions can serve only to furnish Y with hypotheses on which to base her own experiments and resulting learning.

Descriptions of knowledge can benefit only those able and willing to receive them.
These requirements are again obvious, yet every day across the world people mechanically attempt to describe their knowledge to those unequipped or unwilling to learn. These "teachers-with-an-agenda"—parents, spouses, friends, siblings, etc.—ignore all evidence that their "student" is unresponsive and blindly continue their "lessons," often growing increasingly frustrated and blaming the "student" for their frustration.

We cannot make another person learn something.
If a person is unwilling to try to learn something, no one has the power to take over her mind and force it to experiment, accumulate, realize, and master. Thus, *there is no such thing as "teaching someone a lesson."* We can, of course, direct to others a stimulating stream of encouragement to strive and learn. But we cannot control the effect this energy produces, any more than the sun can control the effect of its radiation upon the plants in a garden.

We hinder and retard others' learning by interfering with their accumulating experience-units.
Accumulations consist only of experience-*units*—the coupling of cause and effect. When cause and effect are "delinked," or the natural effect altered by outside intervention, no accumulation based on the

original action can result. This is what happens when Person X, for whatever motive, positions himself between the actions of Person Y and the effects those actions (would) cause. This interference in Y's experiment prevents her from experiencing a cause-effect sequence. Thus is she robbed of the possibility of adding to her accumulations, which alone result in learning. Note that nature never acts in this way—only people do.

We promote and hasten others' learning by encouraging experiments and not interfering.

Only experiments can produce "experience-units"; only "experience-units" can produce accumulations; only accumulations can produce learning. Therefore, encouraging others to experiment and helping them design good experiments—if we are invited to do so—are the best ways to promote their growth. Once an experiment is underway, it remains only to stand clear and let the causes produce their effects. The system works only if we do not interfere with it.

As these axioms make plain, interfering in others' affairs does not work. It does not help them learn things, or hasten their learning, or help them have better lives, or inspire in them respect and affection for us, or lead to their seeking out our counsel and advice. It does, however, provoke resentment, infringe their free will, rob them of experiences that rightly belong to them, and hinder and retard their learning—all while simultaneously agitating ourselves! Clearly, none of these things is in either our own or others' higher interest. So we realize that we need to establish a radically new set of guidelines for our physical, emotional, and mental actions that align them with the MOOB principles. Following such guidelines will enable us to stop interacting with others in agitated and illegal ways that do not work, and to find calm, dispassionate, lawful ones that do.

C. Applying the MOOB Principles to Speech

The four simple "do" and "don't" statements below are all we need to bring our speech in line with the MOOB principles. Each is illustrated by a sample conversation accompanied by an analysis and commentary (in brackets and italics) at the end of each line.

DO give information, advice, or guidance that is freely solicited by others.

> X: I don't know how to transfer music to my phone. Could you show me how? [*Solicitation*]
> Y: Yes. Tap that icon and a menu will appear… [*Lawful guidance (solicited)*]

DO ask if you may offer information, advice, or guidance; offer it if told "yes."

> X: I don't know how to transfer music to my phone. [*A statement, not a solicitation*]
> Y: I do. Want me to show you? [*Offer of guidance*]
> X: Yes, please. [*Acceptance of offer*]
> Y: Tap that icon and a menu will appear… [*Lawful guidance (solicited)*]

DO NOT offer unsolicited advice or guidance.

The offending sentence usually contains *should*, *ought to*, or *need to*. (You need to read some books on Buddhism. You should go to the concert tonight. You ought to become a vegetarian.)

> Y: I see you have a smartphone. You should use the calendar to track appointments. Do you know how to find it? [*Sentence #2 is **unlawful** (as well as **presumptuous**). It is not Y's business to decide how X should use his phone or any of his other possessions, or to tell him so.*]
> X: No. [*A statement, not a solicitation*]
> Y: All you have to do is tap that icon and a menu will appear… [***Unlawful!!** X has not asked Y to teach him how to find his phone's calendar.*]

Here is the same conversation, but with Y asking questions and reacting to X's answers in a lawful way:

> Y: I see you have a smartphone. Do you use the calendar to track your appointments? [*Sentence #2 is now lawful: Y is no longer telling X what to do; he is merely inquiring what he does.*]
> X: No. [*A statement, not a solicitation*]
> Y: Do you know how to find it and enter data? [*Lawful. Y is again merely asking a question.*]
> X: No. [*A statement, not a solicitation*]
> Y: Want me to show you? [*Lawful: another question*]
> X: No. [*Rejection of offer*]
> Y: OK. (Or, "If you ever change your mind, ask.") [*No further attempt by Y. End of conversation.*]

A note about *should, need,* and *ought* is in order here. Often we use these offending words out of an abundance of enthusiasm rather than a desire to control others and impose our will on them. For example, if you tell someone, "Oh, wow, you really need to see this movie" or "You should read this novel," what you probably really mean is, "I saw this film or read this book and I *really* liked it, and I hope you'll like it too." However, there is an easy way to convey your enthusiasm without inadvertently telling the person that he should do something: say simply, "Oh, wow, I saw a great movie last night called ———!" You can even add a description about the cast and the plot, and state your opinion that it is a must-see movie. But just do not tell others that they *should* or *need to* or *ought to* see it. That is rude as well as presumptuous —after all, you do not know for certain what they or anyone else needs.

Do NOT ask to give advice or information, be told "no," and offer it anyway.

    X: I don't know how to use my phone's calendar. [*A statement, not a solicitation*]
    Y: Want me to show you? [*Offer of guidance*]
    X: No, I'm too tired. [*Offer **not** accepted*]
    Y: Oh, you are not. It's really easy. Here, let me show you. [**Unlawful and presumptuous!** *It is not Y's place to tell X that he is not tired, especially after X just said that he was.*]
    X: I really am too tired. [*Offer **not** accepted again*]
    Y: Just tap that icon and a menu will appear… [**Unlawful!!** *X has twice expressly rejected Y's offer.*]

Here is the same conversation, but with Y responding lawfully.

    X: I don't know how to use my phone's calendar. [*A statement, not a solicitation*]
    Y: Want me to show you? [*Offer of guidance*]
    X: No, I'm too tired. [*Offer **not** accepted*]
    Y: OK. If you want me to show you when you're not tired, I'll be glad to. [*Y honors X's wishes and responds with lawful, non-intrusive, open-ended offer.*]

D. Frequently-Asked Questions about Solicitation & Asking

The speech guidelines above often give rise to questions about solicitation and asking. Here are the most common:

What if someone fails to give a direct answer to my question, "May I offer you some advice?"
This happens in one common situation:

   Y: May I offer some advice about your problem? [*Solicitation*]
   X: What is it? [*Not an acceptance*]

Danger—this response is not necessarily an answer to the question. Sometimes it does mean, "Yes, what is it?" But other times it is a suspicious, fence-straddling response that leaves the door open to charges by X—after he hears the advice—that Y is interfering in his affairs. It is easy to avoid the problem by following X's non-committal response with a clarifying question:

   Y: May I offer some advice about your problem? [*Solicitation*]
   X: What is it? [*Not an acceptance*]
   Y: Does that mean "yes"? [*Clarifying question*]

Now X must commit himself. If he answers "yes," he cannot truthfully claim interference if he does not like what he hears. If he answers "not yes" (in whatever form), Y should cease attempting to help. (Of course, X could always answer "yes," then later claim interference. In that case let Y carefully note that at least sometimes when X says "yes," he does not mean it.)

Can't solicitations to help sometimes be unspoken or implicit, eliminating the need to ask?
Yes, invitations and solicitations can be implicit as well as explicit. By enrolling in a class, for example, students implicitly invite the teacher to inform or advise them. Many long-term friendships include the standing request, "If you ever have observations or information or suggestions concerning me, I am always open to hearing them." In all cases, one principle is best and always leads to lawful behavior: if there is any question about whether you have an invitation to advise someone, ask; then you will know for certain. It is always better to try a person's patience by repeatedly asking permission to offer advice, than to violate the law by giving the advice without his permission or against his will.

What if I sense someone needs and wants help, but doesn't ask?
People may indeed want information, advice, or help, yet not ask for it for various reasons. They may be shy or afraid or intimidated, or worried what you or others would think. They may be so confused, or so

little understand the nature of their problem, that they cannot even formulate the right question concerning it. They may not know that you possess the knowledge they need or want.

In these situations it is always lawful to offer them assistance. You can say that you are aware that they seem to be experiencing a problem, and ask if they would be willing to hear your analysis of or advice about it. Many times they will gladly and appreciatively accept your offer and receive your ideas. Never reject the promptings of your higher nature to aid others only because they don't ask—take the initiative and do the asking yourself.

What about the special case of parents and their children?

In countless situations with their young children, the clear duty of parents is to offer advice and guidance, and even to intervene, all without invitation. BUT… They can strive to interfere as little as possible and only when really necessary. They can conduct their interventions courteously and respectfully. They can explain why they considered the intervention necessary. They can assure the child that they have no dictatorial desire to control his or her life. And they can promise to end "intervention-without-invitation" as the child matures. Acting thus, they will be respecting the sovereignty of their fellow human souls who are their children, helping them to learn and grow, and setting an excellent and much-needed example.

E. Applying the MOOB Principles to Mental & Emotional Actions

In Chapter 3 we noted the fact that we harm others through subtle radiations of lower nature energy:

> When people smoke, their lit cigarettes and exhalations fill the surrounding air with toxic chemicals. All those nearby are then forced to breathe this second-hand smoke, to the detriment of their health. An analogous situation exists in the subtle energy world. When aroused, not only do lower-nature energies vibrate within us, but they radiate outward, either inflicting themselves directly on others or creating a toxic atmosphere that others must "breathe." These harmful emanations take numerous forms and produce various effects. (p. 20)

A significant part of failing to mind our own business takes the form of such non-physical radiations of lower energy. Below are listed a number of these harmful interferences, followed by a commentary on them based on the MOOB principles. As you read, I suggest to pause after each and conduct three experiments:

- Recall instances when you did what is described, and try to feel the energy you generated and the agitation it caused you.
- Imagine what it felt like to be the person on the receiving end of your energy radiation.
- Observe how the commentary's "rebuttal ideas," if anchored in your psyche, could prevent future such reactions.

To feel or radiate displeasure, condemnation, or unfriendliness towards others because they refuse to listen to or follow your advice.

But your advice may be useless or unsuited to them, or expressed in a language they do not understand. Even if not, like you they have every right to act as they see fit—as they will.

To condemn others in thought for doing something that (to you) is obviously stupid and not in their higher interest.

To wish that others were less ignorant and would act differently.

But your wishful thinking cannot cause their accumulations to increase, which alone would eventually remove their ignorance and change their conduct.

To think that by making (what to you are) obvious mistakes, others are ruining their chances to learn and grow.

But really these "mistakes" are invaluable and necessary experience-units which are the *cause* of their growth and increased understanding.

To believe and radiate to others the idea and attendant displeasure that their "mistakes" are serious, irremediable, and shameful.

But not only are "mistakes" not irremediable, they are inherently self-correcting. And people should be proud of experimenting; only non-experimenters have cause for shame.

To feel and radiate frustration that others are not serious enough about evolving, and frivol away precious time and resources on unimportant pursuits.

But if you take your evolution seriously and spend your precious time and resources on important pursuits, it is only because your experience-pile is large enough to have taught you the value of doing so. Yet what could this experience-pile be built of, if not countless experience-units which resulted from *not* taking your evolution seriously enough and from frivoling away precious time and resources on unimportant pursuits? So, if others do not live as you do, it is only because *their* experience-pile is not big enough to have taught *them* the value of doing so. But this fact is no cause for frustration on your part, since all of the experiences generated by their "frivolous" attitude accumulate, and eventually, because of those very accumulations, they will change their ways.

- **To indulge the insulting notion that others lack either enough intelligence or potential for intelligence to be able to find their own way.**
  But all their experiments lead inexorably to increased intelligence.

- **To imagine that you are responsible for others' learning and that they cannot learn unless you intervene.**
  But their learning happens because of their own experiments, and your interfering can only hinder and retard it.

- **To think and radiate to others the idea that if their actions have led to their suffering, they have done something bad.**
  But suffering is not bad; it is merely nature's message to an experimenter that an action is in disharmony with a law.

- **To feel and radiate disappointment in someone for being "too smart" to have made a certain "mistake," and wish that he will never make that "mistake" again.**
  But "mistakes" indicate insufficient accumulations. Since the person therefore requires more of a certain type of experience to complete her learning, we should wish for her—and aid her when possible—to have those experiences to the full, and sooner rather than later.

F. The Solution

Two solutions are actually involved here: one for eliminating the agitation we cause ourselves, the other for helping others in an effective but lawful way. Our earlier analyses of the MOOB problem and principles have already touched on most of the elements of both. Let us add what is necessary and summarize all the information.

(1) For dealing with yourself

Inventory the motives that habitually lead you to interfere.

Lower nature ones will naturally be the more common. As an aid to identifying them, review the list of personality types in Section A above to see which might apply to you. Then note as well any higher motivations (originating in either head or heart) that might inadvertently lead to well-meaning but unlawful actions.

Become aware of when you are interfering.

Next, begin carefully to observe your actions to see if, when, where, how, and why you fail to mind your own business. When considering your speech, note how many of your sentences include *you should*, *you ought to*, or *you need to*. Regarding your thoughts and feelings, note if and when you commit subtle-energy-radiation violations. You can refer to the list in the previous section, and be sure to check whether you are radiating *you should* even when you do not say it. Finally, observe the actions of other people to study how they may violate the MOOB principles; this can add to your general awareness of the problem.

Imagine ceasing to interfere.

Once you are aware of how the problem manifests, activate your imagination. Imagine that it is possible to observe people doing whatever they do—conducting (bad) experiments, failing to experiment, experimenting based on faulty hypotheses—and letting them do it without interfering. Imagine how liberating this would be, not to suffer the agitation of a mind constantly thinking about and criticizing others, and emotions not roiling with impatience, frustration, anger, discouragement, anxiety, and the like. Imagine yourself completely trusting that nature's learning system will work fine for others, and how this frees you of the desire to interfere.

Experiment with not interfering.

Finally, test your imagination in action. Seek out those situations in which you habitually interfere, try not doing so, and observe the effects.

Use the previous dispassion techniques in conjunction with this one.

Realistically, most people act on only a small percentage of the advice they receive. So before you offer suggestions or guidance to others, make sure that you (1) have created no expectations that they will take your advice, (2) are prepared instantly to accept the fact of any non-response, and (3) will not regard those non-responses as the least bit serious.

(2) For dealing with helping others

The task here is to radically reconfigure your methods to align them with the principles of nature's learning system, while still leaving room for the full expression of your desire to be of service and share what useful information you might possess.

Always ask permission to offer advice, and respect answers of "no."

We have addressed the permission issue in Section C above; the guidelines there are easy to follow. What is more difficult is truly respecting a "no" answer. To do this, you must not only refrain from giving the advice, but radiate not even the faintest energy of disappointment, disapproval, condemnation, or criticism at others because of their rejection of it. Instead, you must instantly forget the whole matter, and ensure that your attitude of friendliness, cheerfulness, and goodwill toward them remains unchanged and does not skip a beat.

If your mind begins to create agendas for others, stop.

Often when you find yourself negatively reacting to people's unwillingness to hear or heed your advice, it is because you have imagined a whole agenda for them beforehand: "Person X needs to take this, this, and this action to counteract that, that, and that mistake she continually makes and doesn't realize it but I do." So cease from planning what others should do and then brooding over the agenda you have created for them.

When you do offer suggestions, float them out with no "hooks."

Of course, you will often recognize what could help others and be invited by them to share your thoughts. When you do, float out your ideas without any accompanying demands that others should accept them, as in, "OK, I'll tell you how to fix your problem, but I expect you to listen and take my advice." Pressuring others not only provokes resentment, but it interferes with their assessment of the merits of your advice. So present all your ideas in the same undemanding spirit as you would set out bird seed in a feeder, to let the birds eat if, when, and as they see fit.

Express suggestions simply and concisely, then stop talking.

Remember that it is the size of others' experience-pile and their degree of "awakeness" that determine whether they will recognize the usefulness of any advice and act on it. No amount of eloquence, persuasiveness, or repetition will sway the unready, and none is needed for the ready. So keep your suggestions short and simple, then pause and let others' actions tell you into which category they fall.

If others show no interest in your advice, don't try to change their mind.
Resist the temptation to debate and argue with the unresponsive. It is a waste of time and energy, and in no one's higher interest.

If others like your advice and seek help applying it, encourage them to experiment.
Often, people have not thought deeply about nature's learning system and its core principle of experimentation. So when appropriate, couple explanations of the advice with encouragement to apply it using the PLS learning principles:

- Adopt the view of earth-life as a school.
- Regard the situations in their life as a laboratory.
- Use their imagination to design experiments in their laboratory.
- Experiment uninhibitedly, ceaselessly, and in the spirit of fun.
- Banish the notions of "sin" and "mistake" from their minds.
- Ignore the voices of fear, doubt, hopelessness, and discouragement that would stop them from experimenting.
- Exult in knowing that they win anytime they learn something from an experience—even if others consider the experience to be "bad."

Besides being an aid in applying advice, these principles are inspiring and liberating in their own right. Hearing about them will often stimulate others' higher nature, uplifting them and supplying them with the internal propulsion necessary to try out your suggestions.

After speaking your piece, step back and withdraw your influence.
Let others experiment (or not) in their own way and as they see fit, and ask for more input from you if and when they want it. Only thus does real learning happing.

When you interact with others in the seven ways described above, it is not hard to imagine what a beneficial effect it has on them. They feel elevated, awake to new possibilities, newly optimistic. They are grateful for thoughtful, impartial, and encouraging advice. They realize and appreciate that you respect their freedom and autonomy, and that you support whatever experiments they choose. So naturally they begin to seek your advice when they have problems—after all, who would not want a friend and advisor like this?—and spread it to their circle of contacts. Thus do your opportunities to serve and uplift increase, and the good you do ripple outward into the world.

G. Exercises for Minding Our Own Business

This chapter contains an unusually large number of principles, guidelines, suggestions, and methods. The following exercises are constructed using a representative sampling of these. You may prefer to create your own versions using a different combination of the chapter ideas that are customized to your particular problem.

Exercise for dealing with your own agitation
- Pick a situation in which you usually fail to mind your own business.
- Identify the ways in which this happens.
  - In speech, using *should, ought to, need to*.
  - In subtle radiations of criticism, disapproval, condemnation, displeasure.
- Note the harmful agitation this causes you.
  - Frustration, anger, impatience, indignation, irritation.
  - Anxiety, worry, futility, depression, discouragement.
  - Recall how these lower-nature reactions are against your higher interest.
- *Imagine that it is possible to stop interfering*.
  - "I can stop telling others what to do."
  - "I can not care when others are not interested in or reject my advice."
  - "I can calmly let others experiment as they see fit."
  - "I can trust nature's learning system to work without my help."
- Note the effect of this imagining on how you feel.
  - Calmer—mind & emotions no longer agitated by others' lives & choices.
  - Less serious—nothing is wrong; it's OK for others to experiment as they like.
  - More energized—interfering by speech or radiation consumes energy.
  - Freer—not trying to control or pressure others is liberating.

Exercise to promote lawful interactions with others
- Pick a situation in which you habitually fail to mind your own business.
- Identify the ways in which you do this.
  - Fail to ask permission, or do so and be told "no" and give it anyway.
  - Create an agenda for others, then thrust it upon them.
  - Accompany your suggestions with pressure to accept them.
  - Argue and debate with others if they don't accept your advice.
  - After giving advice, interfere in others' experiments applying it.

- Recall the learning system principles that apply to the situation.
  - Others must do their own learning.
  - There is no such thing as "teaching someone a lesson."
  - Interfering hinders and retards others' learning.
  - Encouraging experiments and not interfering in them promotes learning.
- *Imagine that it is possible to align your actions with the principles.*
  - "I can respect answers of 'no' to offers of advice."
  - "I can stop creating agendas for others."
  - "I can float out my suggestions without 'hooks' or pressure."
  - "I can express suggestions simply and concisely, then stop talking."
  - "I can encourage experiments and help others design good ones."
  - "I can step back and let others experiment without interfering."
- Picture the good effects your principle-aligned actions have on others.
  - They get thoughtful suggestions presented without pressure/haranguing.
  - They get encouragement to experiment freely, without limits, in all areas.
  - They suffer no outside interference in or criticism for their experiments.
  - They experience your example of how best to help others.

H. Minding Our Own Business in Action

As is our custom, let us observe our friend Robin, this time as she applies the non-interference principles to the situation with her son. We begin as usual at the point where she contemplates the "F" on his report card. We observe irritation, anger, and frustration in her psyche.

> How could my son let this happen? I've told him repeatedly how important good grades are. I guess I'll just have to show him how to study properly, whether he likes it or not. I am so going to teach him a lesson!

With these thoughts Robin realizes, "Whoa, I have an interference problem." So she reaches for the checklist [following page] she has made for herself and reads through it.

This review calms Robin's hot temper and reminds her of the lawful way to deal with the situation:

> OK. I'm not going to agitate myself by creating some elaborate study agenda for my son and trying to impose it on him. The time for that is past—he is eighteen years old and responsible for his own school life. If he's willing, I'm going to offer suggestions for how to study more effectively, and offer to help him apply them. But I'm not going to pressure him to take my advice, and if he doesn't, I'm not going to walk around the house seething and radiating condemnation at him for not doing so. He will already feel bad about this F, and it would be "soul-discourteous" of me to add to his burden.

> **My "Mind My Own Business" Checklist**
>
> - Am I failing to mind my own business in my speech?
>   - Am I giving others unsolicited advice?
>   - Am I asking to give advice, being told "no," and giving it anyway?
>   - Am I telling others what they need to/ought to/should think or do?
> - Am I interfering with others through subtle energy radiations?
>   - Am I displeased or unfriendly because others refuse my advice?
>   - Am I condemning others for "mistakes" or "bad" experiments?
> - Am I offering advice in the lawful way?
>   - Am I asking permission to advise, and respecting "no"?
>   - Am I refusing to create agendas for others?
>   - Am I floating out my suggestions with no pressure or "hooks"?
>   - Am I expressing my advice simply and concisely, then stopping?
>   - Am I encouraging others to experiment?
>   - Am I withdrawing after advising to let others experiment in their way?

With this attitude in place, Robin talks to her son about the situation. He reluctantly agrees to hear some of her suggestions, expecting them to be accompanied by the usual lengthy and disapproving lecture. But Robin gives her advice cheerfully and briefly, encourages him to experiment with it, offers to help him if and however he needs, and wishes him good luck. He is visibly impressed and relieved.

Two days later he tells Robin, "I tried your suggestion about making note-cards, only I did it in a different way from what you described. And it kind of worked; I made an B- on the quiz today. But I have a chapter test coming and really need to do better. So could you show me exactly how you suggest doing it? ... And Mom—thanks for not browbeating me about how to fix my screw-ups like you have in the past." We observe Robin's reaction:

> Wow, that was really different from past incidents when I would get myself into a tizzy over his problems and try to force my ideas on him! And he obviously feels better, too—appreciative and communicative instead of resentful and closed off. And it's so nice to be asked for help! Now he might actually listen to and consider using what I know that could help him. I just wish I had tried this approach with him from an earlier age.

I. Summary

- The desire to advise others can originate in the higher or lower nature.
- There are lawful and unlawful ways to advise and help.
  - Lawful one—helps without coercion or interference.
  - Unlawful one—trespasses into others' affairs with uninvited advice.
- Seven principles of nature's system govern the lawful process:
  - Everyone must do his own learning (build own experience-pile).
  - We can describe our experience pile to others, but never transfer it.
  - Descriptions of knowledge are not the same as direct experience.
  - Such descriptions benefit only those able/willing to receive them.
  - We cannot make another person learn something.
  - We hinder others' learning by interfering with their accumulations.
  - We aid their learning by encouraging experiments/not interfering.
- Violating these principles harms both ourselves and others.
- We can stop illegal interference in speech by following four rules:
  - Do give information/advice/guidance if others freely solicit it.
  - Do ask to offer information/advice/guidance & offer it if told "yes."
  - Do not offer unsolicited advice ("you should, ought to, need to").
  - Do not ask to offer advice, be told "no," then offer it anyway.
- Illegal interference can also take the form of subtle energy radiations:
  - Displeasure, condemnation, or unfriendliness towards others because they refuse to listen to or follow your advice.
  - Condemnation of others because you disapprove of their choices.
  - Heavy seriousness about others for making "mistakes."
  - All such attacks are an egregious violation of "soul courtesy."
- Helping others in lawful ways benefits ourselves.
  - We avoid anger, frustration, irritation, criticism, worry, etc.
  - We free our minds from undue concentration on others' lives.
  - We remain calm/centered, and thus better able to help when asked.
- Helping others in lawful ways benefits others.
  - They feel elevated, awake to new possibilities, newly optimistic.
  - They receive thoughtful, impartial, and encouraging advice.
  - They receive respect for their freedom and autonomy.
  - They receive your support in whatever experiments they choose.
  - They learn from your example how to help others in the best way.

9

CURBING UNNECESSARY SPECULATION

[In Chapter 7, we briefly touched on this topic as part of the section on "Enemies of Learning." We will now treat it more fully as a stand-alone dispassion technique.]

A. The Problem

We devote much of our thought-life to speculative thinking. We speculate about our own capacities, finances, health, relationships, children, future (Will I ever meet Mr./Ms. Right? I wonder if I'll succeed at this job…). We speculate about others' motives, viewpoints, ideas, thoughts, feelings, reactions (Why did Jack do that? What did my boss mean by that?). We speculate about events or situations of uncertain outcome in the worlds of politics, business, sports, technology, entertainment, etc. It is only when we stop and listen to ourselves and others that we realize how much we speculate and what a habit it is.

As we pointed out in the earlier chapter, a small part of such speculation is useful. It stimulates our growth by generating an impetus to investigate. We think, "I wonder if this idea could lead to a better way of living" or "What might happen if I tried to do this thing a new way?" and we experiment to find out. Clearly, this type of speculation leads to self-knowledge and self-mastery, and thus serves our higher interest.

Most of our speculation, however, does not fall into the "useful" category. Here are some common types, with an example of each:

- We speculate about things that do not matter.
  (How can my neighbor afford that new car? Maybe he…)

- We speculate about questions that speculation cannot answer.
  (I wonder if I could lose weight using this diet…)

- We speculate without possessing sufficient facts.
  (Maybe Jay was kidding, or maybe… [Speaker doesn't know Jay.])
- We speculate instead of asking simple questions.
  (What could Megan have meant? => "What did you mean?")
- We speculate about the future based solely on the past.
  (I'll probably fail at this relationship as I did in all the others.)
- We let speculations morph into beliefs, then regard them as facts.
  (Maybe Rob wants to break up with me. => I believe Rob wants to break up with me. => Yes, Rob wants to break up with me.)
- We try to learn by speculating instead of by experimenting/doing.
  [See p. 84–85 for our earlier analysis of this problem.]

Misusing speculation in these ways harms both our mind and emotions. It squanders our mental energy on purposeless lines of thought. It produces needless motion, clutter, and noise in the mind. It robs us of the mental calm and quiet necessary to register ideas from our higher nature. Emotionally, speculative thinking frequently inflames and energizes the lower nature, generating the very agitation we are trying to eliminate. Speculations about our future, for example, often give rise to discouragement or futility; speculations about other people's motives or intentions may make us angry or resentful; speculations about someone's reactions to us can lead to anxiety or self-doubt.

Many of our speculations also cause us to inflict harm on others. Such speculations produce distorted perceptions of people, which we then project onto them in ways that cause discord, pain, and suffering. This is especially common in close relationships. For instance, a PLS user describes one of her typical "mother speculations" like this:

> I will overreact to something like, say, my fifth-grader's poor result on a maths exam. I start speculating, "Oh no, she'll probably never master maths, so she'll never get into uni, she'll never have a good job, she'll hate her life," etc. From there, I leap to believing my speculations are an imminent reality. Then, based on these "facts," I turn my agitated lower energy on my daughter, trying to head off this "inevitable" sequence of events I've speculated. Naturally, she is bewildered and pained, and afterwards I feel terrible for making her suffer.

Perhaps the biggest speculation problem we encounter is our habit of not stopping the ones that are untestable. We usually have no such problem with testable speculations. Very few of us, for instance, would speculate for long about why our TV remote is not working; we would instead stop, reinsert or replace the batteries, and see if that solves the problem. But let the speculation be untestable, and we tend to persist endlessly in it. This occurs most frequently with "why" speculations, which seem to possess some magical, hypnotic power of ensnaring us with irrational promises of eventual knowing—which never happens. The result is to delay or even prevent our switching from obsessing over the theoretical "why" of a situation to figuring out the practical "how" of addressing it.

To illustrate this problem, consider the response of two women, Mandy and Mindy, to a relationship break-up. Mandy resists the temptation to speculate "why" and focuses on applying the PLS "how" methods. Here is the sequence of her thoughts:

> Why did Lucas break up with me? Is there another woman? Why did this have to happen to me? ... Whoa, wait, wait. "Why" speculations like this won't help me stop all this agitation I feel—anger, resentment, fear, self-pity. How do I break free from this? ... I have to try to apply the dispassion techniques, however hard that it is in the midst of all this pain. ... Accept the fact that regardless of the reason, the relationship is over, and stop wishing that it weren't. Discard all the exploded expectations I created—that the relationship was permanent, that it would survive our incompatibilities, that Lucas would be a certain way. Remember that in the long run, this break-up is not serious, and I don't have to feel serious about it even now. Reflect on and learn from the experiences I had in the relationship, and keep experimenting. Mind my own business, which is to deal with my reactions and situation, not to speculate about Lucas's motives.

By thus directing her thought, Mandy acts in her higher interest and begins calming her agitation. This enables her to think rationally, learn quickly, and regain her equilibrium.

Mindy, by contrast, allows herself to be sucked into the world of "why" speculation. Here is her thought-sequence:

> I cannot believe this. Why did Lucas break up with me? What could he have been thinking? He said there's no one else, but maybe he's lying; why else would he leave me? I am so hurt and angry. [Cries.] There must be another woman. But who is she? Maybe it's Gina, the coworker he's always talking about. Or that Rita woman we met at the pool who I could swear was flirting with him. God, why did this have

to happen to me? It's so unfair and I'm so miserable. I'll always be alone. Why does the universe not want me to be happy? [Sinks into utter despair. Cries uncontrollably.] I'm going to call Carla; maybe she can help me figure out why everything happened. [Carla answers, and she and Mindy begin speculating anew....]

So where has this pursuit of "why" left Mindy? She is not only still agitated and miserable, but even more so. She still has no answers to her questions, and now she is stuck with them reverberating in her mind. She still has not acknowledged the real problem (her own agitation) or applied a single dispassion technique to it (the only way she will remove it). And to top it off, she has dragged another person onto the "speculation train" with her.

These examples illustrate two important facts about "why" speculations. First, note that Mindy's agitation and pain multiplied when her initial, personal speculations (why Lucas broke up with her, who the other woman was) led her down the rabbit hole of existential ones (why the event happened to her, why the universe is against her). Why rabbit hole? Because the starting point of these latter speculations is itself a speculation! For example, the question, "What is the reason for this happening to me?" contains the speculative premise, "Everything happens for a reason." If we are honest, we must admit that however strongly we may think or believe concepts like this—or want to—we do not know for certain whether they are a fact. (It could be that some things happen for no reason related to us.) But what *is* certain is that these existential speculations tend to cause us substantially more harm than do the more mundane kind. In Mindy's case, her (speculative) assumption that the universe possesses the power of bestowing happiness on humans or withholding it from them, leads her to speculate why it has unfairly chosen to do the latter in her case. This speculation results in far more anguish, futility, self-pity, pessimism, despair, depression, etc. than all her "why" speculations about what Lucas did—truly a hell on earth.

Second, note from Mandy's example that to use the PLS and its "how" dispassion techniques, we do not need to know the answers to any "why" questions about people or situations. Such knowledge constitutes no part of how we prevent or remove agitation. Nor do we need to know "why" about any existential question. For PLS users, whether or not things happen for a reason, or circumstances have any meaning, or the universe has any personal interest in or attitude toward us, etc., is irrelevant. Whichever it is, our task and response are the same: meet each situation by (1) applying our knowledge of how not to be thrown into agitation about it, and (2) experimenting to find the best way to deal with it.

B. The Solution

As with the other dispassion problems, the solution to this one employs all the familiar tools: awareness, logic, intervention, imagination.

Take stock of your speculative tendencies and habits.

Consider each common type of speculation listed at the beginning of the chapter and note whether you engage in it, under what circumstances, to what degree, etc. If you do, note specific instances, subjects, and patterns, and the effects produced. Also, listen carefully to others to study the ways they speculate and the effect it produces on them and their contacts.

Become aware of when you begin a speculative line of thought.

Pay attention to when your thoughts or spoken sentences begin with expressions like *Maybe...* or *I wonder...* or *Why would....* Here are examples:

- Will I ever meet Mr./Ms. Right?
- I wonder if I'll be able to learn this new software for my work.
- Why did Paul do that?
- What did Lauren mean by saying that?
- Why would my co-worker think that?

When a speculation begins, ask whether it can ever lead to knowing.

Imagine following the speculation to the logical extreme. Can it ever lead to certain knowledge about the subject? For example, can you know whether you will meet Mr./Ms. Right by speculating about it? Can you know how much money your business will earn this month by speculating about it? Can you know what an MRI will show by speculating about it?

If the answer is "no," accept this fact and stop speculating.

If the speculation is of a potentially purposeful type ("I wonder why this refrigerator is leaking..."), replace it with some practical activity that could lead to knowing (asking questions, researching facts, experimenting, etc.). For all other types, just stop.

Note the damage you can cause yourself if you do not stop.
Observe any lower nature agitation (self-pity, irritation, discouragement, worry, etc.) that the speculation is presently producing, or has already produced. Consider the time and energy you will waste if you let it continue, the undesirable mental and emotional habits you will create, and the harm these agitations could possibly cause others down the road. Consider as well the more profitable higher thinking and feeling you could be doing instead, but won't be if you continue.

If you find yourself speculating "why," shift your focus to "how."
Instead of speculating, say, *why* someone did what he did, direct your attention to *how* best to deal with whatever new facts have arisen as a result of his actions. For example, if Dan's words have provoked agitation in you, focus on how to apply the dispassion techniques to silence the reaction, not on why Dan spoke as he did. Note that every moment you spend theorizing about his (irrelevant) motives will be a moment not spent on your dispassion task, thus prolonging your agitation and delaying your liberation from it.

Cultivate contentment with not knowing why.
It is easy to become hypnotized by and addicted to the idea, "I must always know why." Imagine the opposite concept from this: that in countless instances you do not need to know why, and that you are perfectly happy not to. Then experiment with freeing yourself from this habitual pursuit by not seeking certain information or explanations. See if you do not feel lighter and freer as a result, as you do when you declutter your living space by discarding needless material possessions.

Meditate daily.
Finally, once you study the subject of meditation in Part II, establish a regular meditation practice. Meditation leads to a quieter mind with fewer thoughts—the perfect antidote to endless speculative thinking and the noise it produces.

C. Exercises for Curbing Unnecessary Speculation

Stopping speculation is not particularly complicated: all we really need is to be aware of when we are doing it, and stop. Many readers may find that they need no exercise to accomplish this. Those who do can use the following simple outline:

- Pick a topic or situation about which you are prone to speculate.
- Note the ultimate futility of the speculation.
  - It cannot reveal what will happen in your relationships, job, health, etc.
  - It cannot reveal others' thoughts, feelings, or motives.
  - It cannot reveal the outcome of events or situations.
- Note the agitation that indulging in the speculation would cause.
  - In your mind: clutter, noise, unnecessary motion.
  - In your emotions: anxiety, worry, self-doubt, futility, criticism, etc.
  - In others on whom you would project your speculative conclusions.
- Note the danger of adding existential speculations to a personal one.
- *Now imagine not engaging in the speculation.*
  - Imagine ceasing trying to know what cannot be known.
  - Imagine feeling perfectly contented not to know.
- Contemplate the benefits which results.
  - Calmer—mind and emotions no longer agitated by endless speculation.
  - Lighter—mind liberated from the weight of needless thought-baggage.
  - Freer—can focus on "how" of silencing agitation & addressing situations.

D. Minding Our Own Business in Action

As is our custom, let us now look in on our friend Robin as she applies the no-speculation principles of this chapter to the situation with her son. We begin as usual at the point where she contemplates the "F" on his report card. We observe irritation, frustration, and disbelief in her psyche.

> How could my son let this happen? Maybe he hasn't been doing his homework, even though he claims he has. Or maybe it's his teacher's fault; I know other students have complained about her. But I also wonder if this material is just too hard for him, and he can't understand it, and then he'll never become a doctor! Oh, wait, I bet it's the girlfriend—spending too much time with her and not studying. Whatever it is, this is so distressing. And now I have to deal with this while my father is sick and we're trying to sell our house. Why does everything have to pile on me at once? What did I do to deserve this?

Finally, Robin catches herself and realizes, "I have a speculation problem." So she reaches for the checklist [facing page] she has made and reads through it.

Contemplating these ideas calms her mind and breaks the "speculation spell" she was under.

> **My "Curbing Speculation" Checklist**
>
> - Am I speculating? (Maybe… I wonder … Will I ever…)
> - Can my speculation ever lead to knowing?
> - If not, am I considering my two options?
>   - For testable speculations: stop and shift to research, experiment, etc.
>   - For untestable speculations: stop.
> - Am I remembering the harm that speculations can cause?
>   - Mind: produce motion/clutter/noise; block reception of higher nature.
>   - Emotions: Inflame, energize lower nature; generate agitation.
> - Am I remembering the increased harm of "existential" speculations?
> - Am I remembering to shift "why" speculations to "how" ones?
> - Am I remembering knowing "why" is not necessary to using the PLS?
> - Am I remembering that it is OK not to know why?

OK, yes, I was way speculating, and no, none of it would have led to knowing what happened. For that, all I have to do is wait (without speculating) until I can ask him and his teacher and get the facts. And how crazy was it to speculate that making a single F is certain to prevent my son from becoming a doctor? And I must stop this "Why now?" and "What did I do to deserve this?" silliness. I can't know the answers to questions like this—or if they even have answers! Plus, speculating about them just leads to "poor me" and "this is so unfair," plus prevents me from applying the appropriate dispassion technique to the agitation this situation provoked.

E. Summary

- We speculate about virtually every area of life:
  - Our own capacities, relationships, children, health, prospects, etc.
  - Others' motives, ideas, viewpoints, thoughts, feelings, reactions, etc.
  - Event and situations in politics, finance, business, sports, etc.
- Some speculation is useful and furthers our higher interest.
  - It stimulates our growth by generating an impetus to investigate.
  - It leads us to experiment and learn.
- Most speculation is useless and detrimental, and we misuse it by:
  - Speculating about things that do not matter.
  - Speculating about questions that speculation cannot answer.
  - Speculating without possessing sufficient facts.
  - Speculating instead of asking questions.

- Speculating instead of learning by experimenting and doing.
- Speculating about the future based solely on the past.
- Letting speculations become beliefs, then regarding them as facts.
* Misusing speculation harms our mental and emotional "bodies."
  - It always produces needless motion, clutter, and noise in our mind.
  - It often inflames our lower emotions and generates agitation.
* Failing to stop untestable speculations is the biggest problem.
  - "Why" speculations are the worst offenders.
  - They never lead us to the certain knowing that they promise.
  - They always delay us from focusing on "how" to solve our problem.
* We note two important facts about existential "why" speculations:
  - They can cause us far more pain than our more "personal" ones.
  - Knowing "why" is irrelevant to using the PLS "how" techniques.
* Not pursuing unnecessary knowing serves our higher interest.
  - We are free to concentrate wholly on applying dispassion methods.
  - We feel lighter and freer, as when we declutter our living space.

10

FORGETTING THE PAST

A. The Problem

As we pass through life, our experiences are continuously imprinted on, and retained in, our memory. Having a memory to look back into and consult is obviously crucial to living and learning. Before we act, we can study similar past actions to review what we did, what effect it produced, and whether it was in our higher interest. Then, based on our past experience, we can adjust our present actions to propel us toward the future we envision.

Most of us, however, are not careful to use our memories only in this way. Instead, we pass vast stretches of time during which our attention is pulled backwards and captured by our past—whether recent or distant. We replay images of a billboard we saw two minutes ago, or the meal we had for lunch, or scenes in a movie we saw last week. We relive conversations and interchanges and incidents with other people. We brood over our "mistakes" in a failed relationship, or the unjust treatment we received from our boss, or our frustrated dreams of being a doctor or a dancer. We watch reruns of inner movies of our childhood and events with our parents and siblings. Sometimes we think for a moment about a future possibility, but then spend an hour painfully recalling all the times we failed at that thing, and conclude incorrectly that we will never accomplish it. In all these instances we are like a person riding in the rear-facing seat of a 1960's station wagon: we are looking only at where we have been, and not where we are and where we are going.

Dwelling on the past in these ways is against our higher interest. First, it is a common cause of agitation. Brooding over past errors and regrets can provoke a laundry-list of lower nature reactions: frustration, disappointment, discouragement, futility, anxiety about similar future situations, fear, anger at something someone did, hopelessness, despair, pessimism, self-pity. If our indulgence in this sort of brooding becomes prolonged and habitual, the agitation we create often becomes a permanent state, lurking unrecognized in the background of our psyche and weighing us down. It is impossible to overstate the damage to ourselves that such a habit can cause, not to speak of the misery we suffer from it.

Second, living in the past cripples our capacity to choose and create our future. Every situation, inner or outer, that we encounter in life consists of a set of facts that lie before us. Some of these facts are the result of our past choices. We can view those choices in our memory, but we cannot go back and undo them and re-create the past, any more than we can uncook an egg or unring a bell. What we can do from our vantage point in the present, though, is create the future. But to do that, we must be looking ahead, not behind. We must direct our full attention to surveying the present facts and available possibilities before us, then use our faculties and resources to guide ourselves toward our goals. Needless to say, we cannot and do not do this when our attention is captured by the past. All we do then is miss opportunities and fail to go where we want to be, which adds more regrets to our memory, which pulls us back into the past even more strongly. Thus does our self-inflicted damage snowball.

Third, having our consciousness stuck in the past distorts our perception, even if we are simultaneously looking ahead as described above. Seen through the lens of our past experiences, facts may appear to be non-facts, possibilities may appear to be impossibilities, opportunities may appear to be non-existent. Suppose, for instance, that our attention is captured by our memory of failed relationships, and we fall into brooding over our experiences in them. We recall incidents, conversations, arguments. We relive the pain, suffering, regrets, frustration and futility that we felt. At some point we become convinced that we will never meet the right person, or that we are incapable of being in a successful relationship, or that all members of the opposite sex are untrustworthy and have ulterior motives, or that it is never safe to reveal our real self to any other person, or any other of countless similar ideas. This combination of memory and exclusively past-based interpretations overwhelms every other possible point of view and forms a distorting lens through which we view the world. Once we are looking through this lens, we often fail to recognize that a new person whom we meet in the present may in fact be a good and trustworthy person, or that with him or her there is the real possibility of a compatible relationship, or that in whatever form it takes the relationship offers a golden opportunity to us to break free from our past limitations. Extend this example to every other area of life—career, family, children, finances, health, etc.—and we can see the scope of the danger that this trap poses. Now all of this is not to say that we should not pay close attention to lessons learned from past experiences and incorporate them into our present choices. But we should equally heed the warning given to every investor who consults the historical data for a stock or bond or commodity: "Past performance is not indicative of future results."

Finally, much of the past that occupies our attention consists of a multitude of insignificant images and voices from our recent experience. For example, our mind may jump from a memory of what someone was wearing yesterday, to a snippet of dialogue from a movie we saw, to the meal we ate for dinner, to a task we completed at work, to our child's last report card, and on and on and on. Though none of these topics may provoke any lower-nature agitation or form a distorting lens, while we are indulging them, they still prevent us from being fully present in the present—the only place where life actually happens and from where we shape our future.

So if dwelling in the past is so detrimental, what pulls us so strongly to do it and suffer the consequences described above? Perhaps the most common forces are simply human nature and habit, which constantly pressure us to fixate on something and follow it into the past. For example, while listening to someone speak, our attention may lock onto a sentence we hear and the thoughts or feelings it provokes. Meanwhile, as the person continues to speak more sentences, time flows ahead and the original sentence slips into the past, dragging our captive attention with it and relocating it there. Scenarios like this happen hundreds of times every day, each one often forming links in a chain of successive "attention-hijackings" which lead us far from the present moment.

We are also routinely pulled into the past by failing to apply the other PLS dispassion techniques:

- We failed to accept the fact of some past act or event, and now keep thinking that it should not be so, or wishing that it were not so, or denying that it is so.
- We invented an expectation that someone violated, and now we recall it to resent it and stew about it.

- We forgot the non-seriousness principle, and so we return to some past situation or event to re-experience it and feel serious about it.
- We forgot or ignored the PLS learning and experimentation principles, so now we remember and relive "mistakes"—not to welcome their educational value, extract their lessons, and move on, but to regret them and fret about what a terrible "error" our experiment produced.
- We neglected to mind our own business, so now we dwell on others' past actions, criticize their choices, and brood about what we think they should have done but didn't, or didn't do but should have.
- We failed to curb our speculation, so now our we speculate endlessly why someone did something in the past or what they meant by some past speech.

Thus do we see again why it is called the Personal Liberation *System*: all the parts are interconnected, and each affects the other—by design. Hence the importance of using all the dispassion techniques together.

B. The Solution

For many, being pulled into the past and wandering there for long stretches is an entrenched habit and not easy to break. Therefore, as you experiment with applying the suggestions below, take the long view and work patiently, as much repetition is required.

Determine the scope of your "past" problem and how it affects you.

Inventory your habitual thought topics and note what percentage of them are memory-based. Then identify the nature of the problem associated with each topic: Causing agitation? Distorting view of present? Preventing creating future? Preventing living in present? Thus armed, experiment with applying the suggestions below to reconfigure your relationship with the past, present, and future.

Strive to keep your attention in the present moment.

The ideal is to keep your attention synchronized with the flow of time, so that it is always in the present. As we noted above, habit and human nature conspire to prevent this and instead drag it into the past. Observe and study how this happens in your particular psyche. Try to locate the exact moment when you vacate the present in your interactions with people and situations, and what causes it. Then imagine that it is possible to resist the backward pull, and experiment with how to do it. Whenever you realize that you have slipped up and slipped backwards, apply the next suggestion.

Imagine forgetting the past the instant it becomes the past.
We touched on a corresponding goal in the chapter on accepting facts:

> Once you recognize the existence of a fact, try to accept it instantly. Make a game of seeing just how fast you can adjust your concepts, ideas, images, notions, beliefs, etc.—or even discard them entirely—when you discover that they do not match facts you have encountered. The ultimate goal is to turn on a dime, shrinking the time between when you realize a truth or fact, and when you accept it, to zero. (p. 48)

The goal here is the same: to remove your attention from the past the instant it becomes the past, and forget. For example, suppose you and a friend plan to meet for a walk, but then the friend calls and cancels. Challenge yourself to see how swiftly you can erase the entire incident from your memory. This means to forget not only that the friend cancelled, but *that the plan to walk ever even existed*. When you can apply this principle to all the "pulled-into-the-past" incidents in your daily life, you free your attention to easily and quickly return to the present, unburdened and undistracted by any past influence.

Try to use your memory primarily to consult your experience pile.
The first paragraph of the chapter described the ideal use of memory:

> Before we act, we can study similar past actions to review what we did, what effect it produced, and whether it was in our higher interest.

So once you establish an attention-in-the-present "beachhead," adopt the policy that you will acknowledge past actions that you wish you had performed differently, but quickly shift to what you could do in the present that would mitigate the undesirable effects of those actions. For example, if you have done a wrong to someone, admit it, apologize, and do whatever you can to offset the damage it may have caused and ensure that it not happen again. In this way you waste no energy reliving and regretting the action, but instead direct all of it to reconstruction and moving forward.

Solve "past" problems by applying previous dispassion techniques.
If you find yourself pulled into the past, determine whether you are there because you failed to apply other dispassion techniques. (You can

use the bulleted list on pp. 119-20 as a checklist.) If so, apply the appropriate technique to stop the line of thought and return your attention to the present. Then be vigilant and ready to apply the same technique if you should find the problem topic again arising and threatening to capture your attention.

If you are stuck dwelling on a past "mistake," recall and apply the following learning principles from Chapter 7 to free yourself.

You cannot know things until you know them. Everything you do is an experiment. Experiments produce both positive and negative experience-units. Both types are necessary, none are mistakes, and none are serious. Extract all the learning you can from whatever you did, then leave the husk behind, return to the present, and apply the lesson to enhance your life.

If you find yourself in the past, suspect your perception of the present.

Recall that the past inevitably forms a distorting lens through which you view the present. Whenever such a lens appears, force yourself to look at the lens itself rather than what you see through it. Remind yourself that nothing seen through a distorting lens is seen or interpreted accurately: "facts" may actually be untrue, impossibilities may actually be possible, opportunities may exist where none appear. Use your imagination to picture alternative viewpoints and interpretations to the ones that have arisen. This enables you eventually to "step out from behind" the distorting lens and return to the present, where the view is uninfluenced and undistorted by the past.

When your attention is in the present, keep it facing ahead, not behind.

When you drive a car, you have a rear-view mirror to see behind you, but if you hope to arrive safely at your destination, you dare not do more than periodically glance in it. Instead, you fix your eyes on the road ahead so that you can evaluate and react to the ever-changing circumstances before you. All travel on the road of life requires an analogous attitude and action. Your memory is your rear-view mirror; use it only sparingly and when necessary. Keep your attention in the present so that you can assess life-situations that arise before you, then judge, plan, cause, adjust, and prevent as those situations require. Thus can you avoid missteps that failing to look ahead inevitably produces, and take full advantage of possibilities and opportunities that only a forward-looking awareness can recognize and seize.

Meditate daily.

Finally, once you study the subject of meditation in Part II, establish a regular meditation practice. Meditation is the most effective means available for gaining awareness, control, and direction of your attention, as well as establishing and anchoring it in the present moment. In addition, all the solution suggestions above work better when combined with meditation.

C. Exercises for Forgetting the Past

- Pick a troublesome topic which tends to pull your attention into the past.
- Note what kind of damage that permitting this to happen causes.
  - Throws you into agitation.
  - Distorts your perception of present facts, possibilities, and opportunities.
  - Compromises your ability to choose and create your future.
- Note how such damage is against your higher interest, and why.
- *Now imagine changing your relationship with the past.*
  - Imagine staying in the present, and what it takes to do this.
  - Imagine forgetting the past the moment it becomes the past.
  - Imagine using your memory only to consult your experience-pile and for practical necessities.
  - Imagine always mistrusting the view you see through your "past glasses."
  - Imagine keeping your attention in the present and facing forward.
- Contemplate the benefits which results from these efforts.
  - Calmer—emotions no longer agitated by past sorrows, regrets, "mistakes."
  - Lighter—mind no longer burdened by weight of past thought-baggage.
  - Freer—choices and opportunities no longer limited by past strictures.

D. Forgetting the Past in Action

As usual, we now look in on our friend Robin, this time as she applies the forgetting-the-past principles to the situation with her son. When she contemplates the "F" on his report card, we see a surge of agitation roiling her psyche: frustration, pessimism, despair, futility, etc. The agitation draws her attention backwards into a painful past, and she sinks into a debilitating and distorting meditation about it:

> Oh, no, not again! He's made F's before, and every time it sends both of us into a downward spiral. He feels humiliated and inadequate and

gives up, and I get depressed and frantic about his future. And now it's going to happen all over again! We're both doomed. He'll probably never be able to dig himself out of this hole. And now I have to suffer all over again like all the other times…

Eventually Robin realizes, "I have not had a single thought in the last ten minutes that has not been about the past. This is crazy-land. I have to get out of here." So she finds the checklist she has made for herself and reads:

My "Forgetting the Past" Checklist

- Am I dwelling in the past?
  - Is it causing agitation?
  - Is it crippling my ability to create my future?
  - Is it distorting my view of the present?
  - Is it preventing my living in the present, where life is?
- Am I addressing "past" problem by applying the PLS techniques?
  - Keep returning my attention to the present.
  - Forget the past the moment it becomes the past.
  - Use my memory only for consulting my past experiences.
  - Remember to apply all the other PLS dispassion techniques.
  - Stop looking at present and future through my "past glasses."
  - Stay in present with attention facing ahead, like when driving.
  - Stop and meditate when I've lost control of my attention.

This reminder jars her attention loose from the past and gets her back on the dispassion track.

> Yes, I'm dwelling in the past and it's causing all the problems listed: I'm agitated; I have a (hopefully) distorted view of the future; and I'm not in the present where the problem is, so I can't address it. Yes, part of why I got sucked backwards came from neglecting to accept facts, not expect things, and not indulge feeling serious. But I realize now that neither my son nor I am doomed. His past F's and my turmoil were then; this is now, a brand new moment, in which we both have creative power. From the PLS I understand how to forget the past in the right way. I can recall what I learned from the past F's and how I dealt with it. Then I can leave the past behind, return to the present, and direct my attention ahead to possibilities and opportunities that will address this situation. If I do this, the outcome can be 180 degrees different for both of us.

Her thinking thus clarified and her attitude adjusted, Robin sets about applying the various techniques to silence her agitation and return her attention to the present and re-anchor it there. Then she talks to her son, directing their conversation to the present and how best to deal with the F.

E. Summary

- We have a memory which records and retains our experiences.
- Having this memory is crucial to living and learning:
  - Before we act, we can study similar past actions.
  - We can review what we did and what effect it produced.
  - Then we can adjust our present actions accordingly.
- Yet most of us are not careful to use our memories only in this way.
- Instead, we let our attention be pulled back and captured by our past.
  - We lose ourselves in unimportant and superficial memories.
  - We relive conversations, interchanges, incidents with others.
  - We brood over past "mistakes," frustrations, resentments.
  - We watch reruns of inner movies of our childhood.
  - We project past limitations onto the future.
- Dwelling in the past in these ways is against our higher interest.
  - It causes agitation—futility, pessimism, self-doubt, frustration, etc.
  - It cripples our capacity to choose and create our future.
  - It distorts our perception of facts, possibilities, and opportunities.
  - It prevents us from living in the present, where life happens.
- Despite these consequences, we let ourselves be pulled backwards:
  - By human nature and habit.
  - By failing to apply the other dispassion techniques.
- We can solve our "past" problems by:
  - Inventorying them to become aware of their nature and extent.
  - Striving to keep our attention in the present.
  - Forgetting the past the instant it becomes the past.
  - Using our memory primarily to consult our experience pile.
  - Making sure to apply the other dispassion techniques.
  - When in the past, suspecting our perceptions to be distorted.
  - When in the present, directing our attention forward, as in driving.
  - Meditating daily to help control the attention/direct it to the present.

11

CONTROLLING SPEECH

A. The Problem

As we saw in Chapter 2, the contents of our psyche—thoughts, viewpoints, attitudes, motivations, feelings, desires, instincts, etc.—are a mixture of our higher and lower natures. As a physical expression of those contents, speech powerfully directs those energies, stimulating both ourselves and others. When our speech is regulated and under the influence of our higher nature, this stimulation is useful. We express our best qualities, strengthening the higher functioning of our mind and feelings. We use words imaginatively and economically to express clear thoughts and "soul emotions." We inspire and encourage others, shed light on their experiences and problems, and lift their burdens. People seek out our company for the quality of our conversation.

When motivated by our lower nature or acting from mindless habit, however, we misuse speech in numerous ways. Here are the most common:

- **We often speak uneconomically.** We speak when it is unnecessary or inappropriate. We use fifty or a hundred words, when five or one would do. We explain ourselves when it is not necessary.

- **We often speak thoughtlessly.** We engage in silly chatter. We start speaking before we know what we want to say. We say things that are exaggerated or untrue. We talk about subjects that do not merit comment. We fail to adapt our speech to our listener.

- **We talk excessively about ourselves and our ideas**.
  We dominate conversations, turning them into monologues about ourselves and preventing back-and-forth dialogue. We talk about

subjects of no interest to anyone else. We fail to listen to others or consider their viewpoint.

- **We argue.** We rush out into verbal battles with people who are not listening to us or considering our ideas, and whose opinions we will never change. (In fact, arguing usually confirms or even hardens their opinions.) We waste our strength debating points of no importance, all the while deteriorating the poise and tone of our mind.

- **We speak unkindly.** We criticize. We engage in gossip and innuendo. We attribute wrong or evil motives to people and groups. We listen to speakers who attack and demean others in a hateful, divisive spirit, then allow our own speech to parrot theirs.

- **We sometimes fail to speak when prompted by our higher nature**, due to fear of what others may think, lack of trust in our own perceptions, etc.—all lower-nature qualities.

Misusing speech in these ways produces a variety of detrimental effects to ourselves and others. One effect is to provoke or strengthen emotional agitation, whose harm we have traced through ten dispassion chapters. Another, resulting from speech's close relation to thought, is to fill the mind with noise and needless motion, preventing us from achieving and preserving the mental quiet necessary for meditation—the other half of the PLS and the subject of Part II of this book. A third is to drain our energy and frazzle our nervous system, making it that much harder to practice both dispassion and meditation. Naturally, all these effects of ungoverned speech overlap and occur simultaneously in all these realms—mental, emotional, and physical. Thus control of speech is an essential technique for both halves of the PLS, as well as our basic physical well-being. Let us investigate the most important problems that failing to govern our speech causes.

Our speech increases agitation already present.
Where dispassion is concerned, our misuse of speech tends to feed and strengthen lower emotions, often far beyond their original intensity. A typical sequence goes like this: emotional agitation of some kind arises, which we then voice in agitated speech, which in turn inflames our emotions, etc., and we find ourselves sucked into a downward spiral of our own creation. Here is an example as described by a PLS user:

Often I will become irritated at something my daughters have done. Initially, the irritation is mild. But as soon as I open my mouth and start talking to them about what they've done wrong, that small spark of irritation explodes into a firestorm of anger that spirals out of control, until I'm yelling and screaming at them. Then at some point I stop talking, and right away the anger begins to subside. Then I realize that my speech is causing all the increased agitation, like pouring gasoline on a fire. So now I have adopted the policy that when I feel a budding irritation at something, I will not open my mouth until I can think about that topic without feeling any irritation. That way I avoid hurting myself by inflaming my lower nature, and my daughters by screaming angrily at them over something that I could address calmly and non-seriously.

Note that this same phenomenon happens with thoughts and speech. The two stimulate each other, so that our thoughts provoke us to speak, which spawns more thoughts, which we express in more speech, ad infinitum. Thus do we inadvertently feed our lower nature by reinforcing undesirable emotions and overstimulating our mind, in both cases through feedback loops created by our uncontrolled speech.

Our speech generates agitation where none previously existed.

Instead of agitation inciting us to speak, as in the example above, the reverse can happen as well. We can begin talking about a person or situation about whom or which we feel no present agitation, then suddenly find our voice rising with the indignation or anger or criticism that our speech has aroused. And when we stop talking, the agitated state that we have talked ourselves into, remains.

Again, this same reverse phenomenon occurs with speech and thoughts. We can start out with our mind calm and focused, then launch into an episode of unregulated speech. Presently our mental quiet vanishes and is replaced by a multitude of noisy thoughts, whose reverberations last long after our speaking ends. And often this mental agitation will be accompanied by unwanted physical effects: fatigue, a wired-up nervous system, a headache, insomnia, and so on—all courtesy of our excessive speech, and all crippling to our ability to meditate satisfactorily.

Our speech lacks economy.

We addressed the particulars of this issue in the first bullet point above. Here is an example taken from real life (with the names changed) illustrating this all-too-common problem:

Joy: I forgot about sending the CDs to you. Do you still want them?
Amy: Oh, well, don't inconvenience yourself, but I was wondering what it would be like to hear them, because they sound so interesting. But I don't want you to have to go out of your way. Is the post office close to your house? I know how much I hate having to go to the post office when the traffic is so bad and it's hot. But if you don't mind, don't make a special trip or anything, just whenever you find time, but *I really would like to have them* so I could listen to them. I think they would really help me.

Note that Joy's question can be answered in one word, yet Amy's answer contains 103 (!), of which only the six in italics directly answer the question. It is tiring just to *read* Amy's response, much less to have to *hear* it. Consider the cumulative harmful effect on her mind and nervous system, as well as those of her listeners, if all her responses are like this. And experience suggests that Amy will be the loudest complainer—probably in a torrent of agitated speech—when, realizing the need to control her mind, she tries to meditate but meets with fierce resistance which her own habit of unregulated speech has helped to build into her mind.

Note how light and uncluttered the exchange could have been with a different response from Amy:

Joy: I forgot about sending you the CDs. Do you still want them?
Amy: Yes, I do, thanks!
Joy: I'll send them in tomorrow's mail.

Our speech inflicts harm on others.

Non-stop talking acts as a verbal machine gun, assaulting others' ears, rattling their nervous system, and disturbing their mind—especially if they are sensitive types who soak up vibrations from the outside. Here is how one PLS user describes such an incident:

I noticed that my co-worker (I'll call her Jenny) looked stressed. I had work to do, but out of concern I initiated a conversation that began as follows:

Me: Oh dear, Jenny, you look upset. What's wrong?
Jen: It's my mom: she's had a long history of depression, and we finally had to put her in the hospital yesterday. ...

If she had stopped right there, everything would have been fine: I would have known the immediate cause of her strife and asked if I could do anything to help. But then she proceeded to tell me about her aunt's unruly cats she had to house-sit, texts to her boyfriend from his former girlfriend, her burden of having to move house, her mom's unfair demands, her kids' problems in school, and much more. After I stood there listening to her monologue for ten or fifteen minutes—with no end in sight—I started to feel tired. I yawned. My head began throbbing. I could no longer think clearly. I felt my energy draining away. It was as if all her agitation was migrating via her speech into my body and psyche and taking it over, and I couldn't stop it. Though I feel bad saying it, I just wanted to get away from her, and looked for any excuse to do so. I regretted asking her what was wrong, and I don't want to ask her again in the future, even if I feel my usual sympathy towards her and would naturally want to express it via enquiries about her well-being.

Our speech is full of unnecessary explanations.

Some of us devote a great portion of our speech to explaining ourselves to others. Here is an example, again taken from real life and with the names changed:

> Roy: Do you ever have occasion to come to California?
> Alan: When my mother was alive I used to come there from time to time, even though I didn't like to. Then she got sick and I had to come all the time, and that was really terrible. After she died, my brother lived there for a while, and we would come to see him. But then he moved to Ohio because he got a new job. He was the last of my family to live in California, so now I don't ever come there.

Along with violating the principle of economy, Alan subjects Roy to a lengthy, unsolicited, and unnecessary explanation of his travel history. Note that he could have briefly answered "no" and let Roy choose whether to follow up with "why," like this:

> Roy: Do you ever have occasion to come to California?
> Alan: I used to, but not any more.
> Roy: (Optional) Oh, how come?

The tendency to explain ourselves excessively and compulsively arises from two closely related motives: (1) we think not only that other people expect an explanation for all of our thoughts, feelings, and actions, but that it would be impolite and inconsiderate not to offer it; and/or (2) we have a morbid fear of being misunderstood and are desperate to ensure that others have not a single incorrect idea about us. Yet careful analysis shows the fallacy and futility of these two motives, as well as the self-inflicted agitation they cause us.

In the first instance, the idea that others expect us to explain ourselves, much less that they would consider it rude if we did not, is merely one that we invent and is rarely true. Far more likely is that others expect no such thing, and that if they consider anything rude and irksome, it is our falsely attributing to them this non-existent expectation, then subjecting them to a superfluous, time-wasting explanation based on it.

In the second case, people can and do form all manner of ideas about us and others without the slightest concern for whether the ideas are true. They make up concepts about us, interpret our words to fit their preconceptions, deny clear evidence and facts about us, refuse to believe us, etc.—and there is nothing we can do to control any of this. Therefore, rushing out to try to correct every inaccuracy about us—real or imagined—that others may invent is an impossibility and a fool's errand.

Acting on these motives is a powerful generator of agitation and stress. Our thought-life turns into a meditation on the contents of others' psyches. We speculate about what they expect and what would offend them, about what misconceptions they have about us and may be gossiping to others about. We then waste time and energy crafting detailed explanations where none are expected or wanted, and indulging fear, worry, and anxiety about being misunderstood. Eventually, all this pours out in speech, strengthening our lower nature and binding us ever more tightly to it.

B. The Solution

The solution to most speech problems is nothing more than to stop speaking in certain ways. The most effective way to accomplish this is by conducting a series of simple experiments. As usual, the first step in the process is awareness. So begin by inventorying your speech habits and identifying your problem areas using the previous section's bullet points (pp. 126-27) as a checklist. For substantial speech-control problems, listening to a recording of yourself talking in selected settings can be quite useful. Once you have identified the problems (and noted the situations in which they commonly arise), study the corresponding entries below for methods of addressing them.

Refrain from agitation-strengthening or -inducing speech.
Recall the solution devised by the PLS user in an earlier example:

> I have adopted the policy that when I feel a budding irritation at something, *I will not open my mouth until I can think about that topic without feeling any irritation* [italics added]. That way I avoid hurting myself and my daughters. (p. 128)

Experiment with refraining from voicing your agitation and instead direct your energy and attention to applying the appropriate dispassion techniques to silence it. This of course does not preclude communicating the fact of the agitation to others, or describing it to them, or discussing the issues involved, if it should be in your higher interest to do so; that is altogether different from expressing it in agitated speech.

Experiment, too, with refraining from talking about subjects likely to induce or reawaken agitation. For example, do not recount to a friend the irritation you felt yesterday with your husband, or the frustration you felt last week with your co-worker, and thus become irritated or frustrated all over again. Such restraint ensures that your speech supports your attempts to practice dispassion and does not hinder it.

Speak economically and thoughtfully.
The violations of these two principles are many and varied, but all share a common feature: the only real method for stopping them is to start doing their opposite. Here are suggestions to experiment with:

- Speak only when it is necessary or appropriate.
- Speak concisely, using the fewest number of words possible.
- Answer questions directly, without wandering off on tangents.
- Speak accurately and truthfully, without exaggeration.
- Pause before speaking to think what you want to say.
- Adapt your speech to your listeners.

Take care not to harm other people with excessive speech.
When you become aware of speaking intensely or at length to someone, be attentive to signs (facial expressions, body language, etc.) that you might be "speech machine-gunning" them and causing them discomfort. If it appears that you are, experiment with tapering off on the quantity and/or intensity of your speech and observing the results. Even better, ask them directly: Am I going into too much detail? Am I talking so much that it is tiring you out? Is this subject not really of

interest to you? Then you will know and can make any necessary adjustments, and they will be grateful for your sensitivity and consideration.

Stop explaining yourself unnecessarily.
In the "Speculation" chapter we saw that we could be content while not knowing various "why's" about people, situations, and the world. Apply the same principle to explanations to others: imagine that it is possible to be happy and unagitated while not explaining to others various "why's" about yourself, or even while freely letting them misunderstand you. Then begin experimenting with ceasing to explain yourself unless asked. For example, if the answer to a question is "no," merely say "no" and nothing else; if "yes," the same. Observe whether others appear to have expected an explanation or thought you rude for not offering one (hint: probably not). Note the energy you save, the agitation you avoid, and the mental quiet you preserve.

When you perceive that others have misconceptions about you, experiment with not rushing out to correct them. Note that you already have a full-time job dealing with yourself and your life, and do not need a second one playing endless whack-a-mole with misconceptions that you did not create and do not belong to you. Trust that those who are truth-seekers will eventually adjust their conceptions based on facts they uncover themselves. And realize that the non-truth-seekers will continue creating inaccuracies no matter how many "mole-whacks" you administer, so save your energy for worthier causes.

Refuse to argue.
If you feel your lower nature pulling you to initiate an argument situation, check your motivations to see if you can avoid it by applying other dispassion techniques. Here are some examples; note that speaking based on any of these motives is likely to provoke an argument with your interlocutor:

- Accepting facts—"I just can't accept that V could believe something this ignorant; I'll explain it again to her."
- Expectations— "Surely I can expect that if I explain the issue to W, he will change his wrong idea."
- Seriousness—"Because I feel really serious about this topic, I need to debate X about it."
- Learning—"Someone needs to teach Y a lesson about this, so I will explain it to him."

- Minding your own business—"I know the truth about this matter and therefore I am going to lay it our for Z whether she wants me to or not, to correct her thinking."

If you find yourself already in a conversation with someone who insists on beginning an argument, experiment with simply declining to reciprocate and remaining silent. Imagine that you can be content and unagitated while letting people be misinformed and/or think that they "win" debates, and experiment with doing so. Observe the beneficial effects of your non-speech on your emotional and mental calm, as well as that of your body and nervous system.

Speak fully and uninhibitedly when prompted by the higher nature.
An essential part of regulating speech is to recognize appropriate times to use it, and do so. So when you register a higher-nature impulse to speak, give it free reign and do not hold back. If many words are required, use them. Remember that higher-nature energy stimulates, inspires, heals, etc., so that when expressing it you can speak at length without tiring yourself or others.

Do not go overboard and over-regulate your speech.
Take care not to push speech regulation to the point of unnatural suppression and thereby turn yourself into a boring conversationalist who is no fun to be around. You can apply all the guidelines for economical and harmless speech while still continuing to speak about interesting topics in an uplifting way. It is simply a matter of finding the proper balance through experimentation.

Meditate daily.
Finally, once you study the subject of meditation in Part II, establish a regular meditation practice. Meditation has a powerful effect on speech regulation, since the fewer thoughts and quieter mind that it produces leads to fewer words and a quieter voice (and vice versa).

C. Exercises for Controlling Speech

- Pick a speech regulation principle that you feel prone to violate.
- Note the people and situations likely to be involved.
- If you had past violations with those same people/settings, recall them.
  - Note how the violation began and what you said/did.
  - Note the harm caused: mental noise, emotional agitation, physical fatigue.

- Note the detrimental effect it may have caused to others.
  - Note what kind of speech regulation could have avoided the problem.
- *Now imagine regulating your speech in future similar situations.*
  - Imagine how you would speak or refrain from speaking.
  - Imagine feeling perfectly calm and contented acting thus.
- Note the beneficial effects that this speech regulation would produce.
  - In your mind: fewer thoughts, less noise and motion, more quiet.
  - In your emotions: freedom from agitation of all kinds.
  - In your body: calm nervous system, less fatigue, more energy.

D. Control of Speech in Action

Let us again observe our friend Robin, this time as she applies the speech-regulation principles to the situation with her son. When she contemplates the "F" on his report card, we see a surge of instinctive agitation in her psyche: frustration, anger, disappointment, disbelief, etc. When her son arrives home, she unloads her agitation on him in agitated speech:

> What is this F about ?! You don't have any business making an F! What are you doing in your room all night when you say you're studying? You're spending too much time with your girlfriend. You're going to ruin your life if you don't pass this course! Do you want to end up living under a bridge?

After a lengthy argument, her son goes up to his room and Robin's agitation finally dies away. But an hour later she has the impulse to call her friend Sally to complain about the F and her son's behavior. Just as she is dialing the number she realizes, "Wait a minute, I have a speech problem. Earlier I failed to control my tongue, and now I'm about to do it again." So she aborts the call and instead consults the checklist [following page] she has made for herself:

This "time-out" resets her mind and gets her back on the dispassion track.

> OK, now I see what I did and was about to do. By yelling at my son I inflamed the agitation I already felt and inflicted it on him. I initiated a stupid argument that solved nothing and helped neither of us. I made a bunch of exaggerated statements that were not true. All these actions made my agitation worse and hurt me. And when I had finally calmed down, I almost let myself talk my way back into the same agitation. How dumb would that have been?

> **My "Speech Control" Checklist**
>
> - Am I violating the law of economy of speech?
>   - Am I speaking only when it is necessary or appropriate?
>   - Am I using the fewest number of words possible?
>   - Am I explaining myself unnecessarily?
> - Am I failing to think before I begin speaking?
>   - Am I clear about what I am going to say?
>   - Is the speech true?
>   - Is it adapted to the person to whom it is addressed?
>   - Is the speech about something that ought to be said?
> - Is my speech increasing already-existing agitation?
> - Is my speech inducing new agitation? Re-inflaming old?
> - Is my speech harming others?
> - Am I arguing?
> - Am I failing to speak when prompted by my higher nature?

Thus sorted out, Robin applies the various PLS techniques to silence her agitation (accepting facts, removing expectations, experimenting, minding her own business, etc.). Then she summons her son and has a calm conversation to troubleshoot his problem with him to see how he could best solve it and she could best help.

E. Summary

- Speech powerfully expresses and directs the energies in our psyche.
- We use speech beneficially when it expresses higher-nature energy.
  - We express our best qualities, thoughts, and "soul emotions."
  - We strengthen the higher functioning of our mind and feelings.
  - We stimulate, inspire, encourage, and heal others.
  - We shed light on their problems and lift their burdens.
- We misuse speech when it expresses our lower nature.
  - We speak uneconomically or thoughtlessly or unkindly.
  - We talk excessively about ourselves and our ideas.
  - We argue and over-explain ourselves.
  - We fail to speak when prompted by our higher nature.
- This misuse of speech harms ourselves.
  - It provokes or strengthens emotional agitation.
  - It fills our mind with noise/prevents our achieving mental quiet.
  - It drains our energy and frazzles our nervous system.

- Our misuse of speech can also harm others.
  - We machine-gun them with excessive speech, draining their energy.
  - When our speech expresses our lower nature, it stimulates theirs.
- We can eliminate these misuses by carefully regulating our speech.
- Regulation involves nothing more than to stop speaking in certain ways.
  - Refrain from agitation-strengthening or -inducing speech.
  - Take care not to harm other people with excessive speech.
  - Speak economically and thoughtfully.
  - Stop explaining yourself unnecessarily.
  - Refuse to argue.
  - Speak fully and uninhibitedly when prompted by the higher nature.
  - Do not go overboard and over-regulate your speech.
- We learn to apply these methods through experimentation.

Part II
Meditation

12

THE BASIS OF MEDITATION

A. Introduction

It is a common experience for people to try meditation, but have unsatisfying results because of vague or mistaken notions about what its purpose is and what they are supposed to be doing. So before we present the PLS meditation, let us investigate in detail the science behind it. Then when we introduce the actual techniques, we will understand the PLS view of the human psychological system and know exactly what we are trying to accomplish within it.

B. The Self and Not-Self

Throughout our study of dispassion and dispassion techniques, we focused our attention on our higher and lower natures and their qualities and energies. To understand the practice of meditation, we must shift our focus to a second fundamental human duality: Self and not-self.

We all experience both changing and unchanging aspects of ourselves. Our physical body constantly changes; its cells are dying and being replaced all the time. The same phenomenon occurs in our "emotional body" and "mental body": our feelings, emotions, and desires constantly change, as do our thoughts, ideas, concepts, and beliefs. If we compare, say, our five-year-old self with our present one, not only are we starkly aware of this fact, but we probably shake our head and think to ourselves, "I can't believe I ever thought that or wanted that."

Yet in the midst of these constant physical, emotional, and mental changes, we experience at our core an unchanging sense of identity or "I" that is unaffected by externalities. Even the most extreme changes in the bodies we inhabit—radical new beliefs, transformed emotional patterns, amputated limbs—do not alter this core "I." This fact leaves us with the unavoidable conclusion that our self is something different from our body, feelings, and thoughts. For simplicity's sake, we will use the terms *Self* and *not-self* for the two poles of this duality, and define them thus:

- *Self*: the enduring, unchanging sense of identity or "I"
- *Not-self*: the changing mind, feelings, body, and outside world

Despite our recognition of this basic duality, we often confuse Self with not-self, a phenomenon we might call *false identification*. It causes us to mistake some thought, feeling, or physical sensation (not-self) that we temporarily *have*, for who we permanently *are* (Self). Here is an example:

> During high school, Alice has a string of bad teachers and bad experiences in her academic subjects. As a result, she carries into adulthood the idea that she has a flawed, inferior intelligence, and she is hounded by feelings of being a failure and a loser. Finally, despite all her lower-nature thought and feeling, she decides to enroll in university and pursue a degree. There, she finds exceptional teachers who explain math and science and literature to her, and over time she realizes that she—her real Self—has always had the capacity to understand these subjects, even while she confused this Self with a swarm of false ideas and feelings of inferiority, self-doubt, and limitation masquerading as that Self.

This phenomenon of false identification is *the* central problem of human life. Nothing causes more pain and bondage than confusing our identity (Self) with an oppressive feeling or untrue idea (not-self), and nothing is more exhilarating and liberating than realizing that our real Self is not that feeling or idea, and never has been.

The whole purpose of meditation is to solve this problem, to enable us to dis-identify with the various false "selves" that arise in our thought and feeling, and locate and identify with the real Self that lies behind them. This dis-identification process corrects a tragic error that afflicts so many: thinking that we are by nature somehow weak or bad or flawed, when it is only our habits, desires, and thoughts that are ever so, and not our Self.

C. The Human Psychological Apparatus

The two fundamental dualities of the PLS—Self and not-self, higher and lower nature—are housed in the psycho-physical mechanism in which we all live. To learn and practice meditation requires us to understand the structure of this apparatus and how our awareness operates within it. To explain this, we will supplement our usual analysis with a visual model illustrating the location of the two dualities, the pathways of access to them, and the dynamic relation between them. Our analysis will consider four main factors—ourselves (human beings), the outside world, our inner psyche, and the spiritual world—and study the relation among them.

1. The outside world

This consists of people, places, things, events, circumstances, etc., in our immediate environment, plus those we know of second-hand through various avenues.

2. Ourselves, human beings

Two factors in ourselves are crucial to meditation: an "attention" or "awareness" which we continuously focus or place somewhere, and a system of centers (or *chakras,* if you prefer the Sanskrit term) through which we access the various aspects of our psychological system. We might picture our attention as an inner "eye" which we direct at thoughts to "see" them, and an inner "hand" which we extend to feelings to "touch" them; and the centers as "doors" which open into different realms and through which we send and recall our attention. For the PLS meditation purposes, we need to consider only four of these center-doors: crown, forehead, heart, solar plexus.

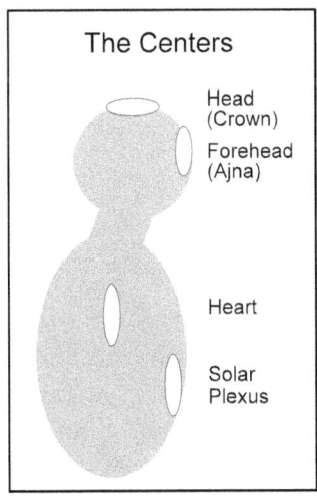
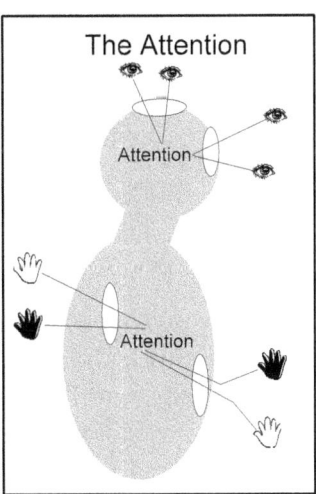

3. Our inner psyche

In our model we will represent our interior psychological world as a cylinder divided into two halves:

- The lower half is the realm of desires, feelings, and emotions, which we perceive horizontally through the solar plexus center/door.
- The upper half is the realm of thoughts, images, memories, beliefs, concepts, etc., which we perceive horizontally through the forehead center/door.

Many people find it helpful to imagine these realms as made of subtle energy-substance and containing actual "thought-forms" and "emotion-forms" that they can perceive with their inner awareness. For example, when we think of a material object like a house or landscape, we construct a tiny image or replica of that object that we view with our inner eye; when we think of other people, we create miniature portraits of them. All such thought-images remain in our mental realm until we remove our attention from them, shift it to another subject, and repeat the process. The same phenomenon exists in the emotional realm. Although the "forms" our feelings and emotions take may be far vaguer than our mental "thought-forms," they are nevertheless quite defined waves of swirling energy that we feel with our inner sense of touch.

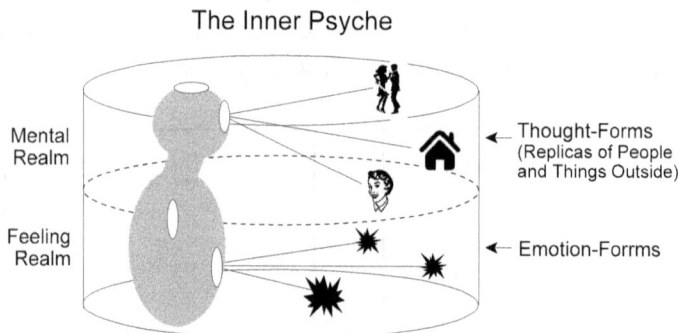

The Inner Psyche

Although the psyche-cylinder in our model has separate designated mental and emotional "home areas," in life our thoughts and feelings occur together and commingle with each other. For example, we may think of what we would do if we won the lottery, and simultaneously have an aching desire to win it; or recall mental images of a relationship break-up, and experience a surge of charged and painful feelings about it. Further, the two energies inevitably react upon and provoke each other. In the relationship example, it was our thoughts that initially aroused our feelings, which incited more focused thoughts, which stirred up more intense feelings, ad infinitum. But of course it could have been feelings that arose first and started the chain reaction, to the same end. The result of this commingling is a unified, hybrid realm which certain schools of thought refer to as "desire-mind" (*kama-manas* in Sanskrit). This realm is home not only to simple combinations of worldly desires and thoughts as in the examples above, but also to complex structures like our ego/personal "I" and the mask we present to the world.

Before we add the spiritual realm to our model, let us pause and summarize what it contains so far:

- The psyche-cylinder is the home of the lower nature (desire-mind).
- The ever-changing contents of this psyche-cylinder (plus of course the outside world) are the not-self.
- The psyche-cylinder and the outer physical world constitute our horizontal, outward, mundane, foreground life.
- We contact this foreground life through our forehead and solar plexus center-doors, which are wide open and fully utilized by most people.

Here is a "zoomed out," big-picture version of how our model looks with these four facts highlighted:

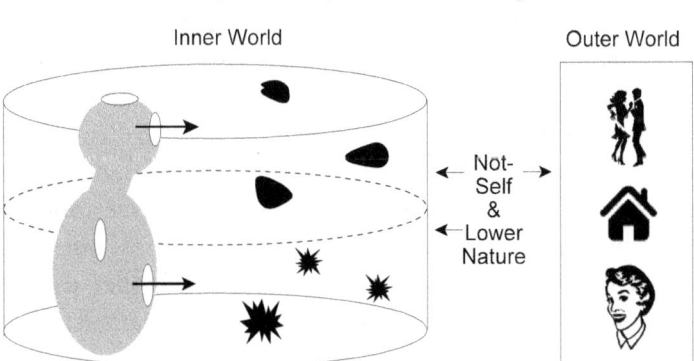

Our Horizontal, Outward, Mundane, Foreground Life

4. The spiritual world

The many religions and philosophies refer to this world by various names: Spirit, One Reality, The Absolute, The Unmanifest, *Brahman*, *Atman*, God, No-thing. They also teach that all humans contain a direct link to this spiritual energy, and that this energy *is* their Self-Identity and higher-nature qualities. In our model we will place this realm of spiritual energy above ourselves and our psyche-cylinder, and represent its connection to each person as a descending funnel, like this:

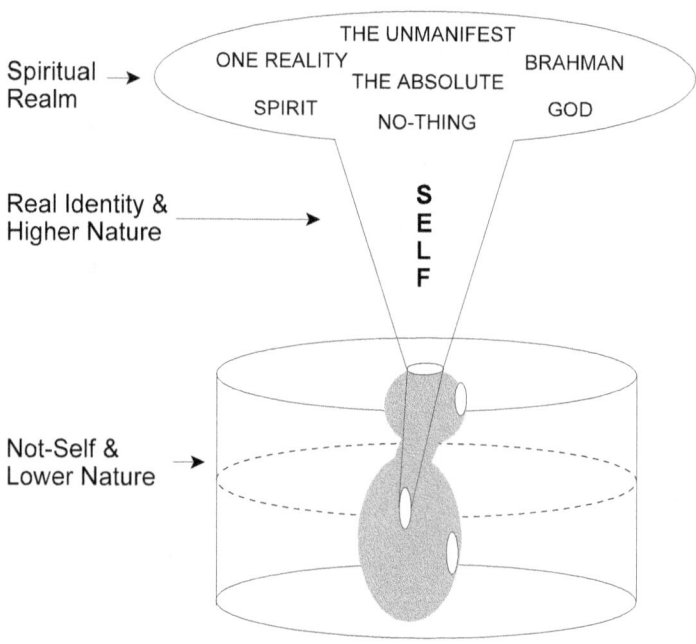

As we can see, this "spiritual funnel" or Self enters vertically through the crown center-door (*brahma-randhra* in Sanskrit, from *Brahman*, spirit + *randhra*, aperture, hole). This center is located both within the middle of the head and in the space above it. (It is this fact that accounts for statues of Buddha with a domed head, or paintings of Christian saints with a halo.) When this crown door is open, we can look vertically "upward" into the spiritual realm and perceive another world above and beyond the mundane one experienced by our individual separated self. This is the world of the Self and higher nature. This direct experience of the Self reveals certain striking characteristics about it:

- It is vividly and irrefutably *real*, and by contrast makes our thoughts, feelings, and the outer world seem dream-like and unreal.
- It is calm, serene, quiet, still, unagitated.
- It is simple and spacious when compared to the crowded complexity of the "psyche-cylinder-world," with the latter's agitated kaleidoscope of images and feelings.
- It is distinct from and unaffected by the mundane world, just as a movie screen is unaffected by the images projected onto it.
- It is the location and source of all our intuitions, insights, and realizations—our light-bulb, "ah-ha!" moments. Note that, as illustrated below (left), the light bulb is located in the Self (funnel), *not* in the mind (cylinder): intuitive realizations may be followed instantly by thoughts derived from them, but thought is not their source.

Having entered through the crown center, the "spirit-funnel" ends in our heart center, its anchor point or seat in our psychological system. When this door is open, we experience and radiate higher nature feeling-energy—"soul emotions" like compassion, inclusiveness, oneness, and selfless universal love, as well as feelings of freedom, independence, and confidence. The illustration below (right) depicts these facts.

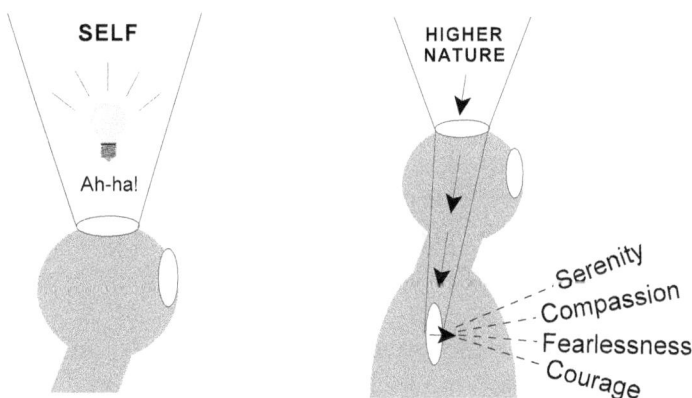

In the previous section, we noted how in the lower nature realm our thoughts and feelings are commingled and linked through the forehead and solar plexus centers. A similar phenomenon occurs in this spiritual part of our being: our higher intuitive insights and our "soul emotions" are commingled and connected through our crown and heart centers. For instance, a profound insight or realization about another's psyche or path may flash in our head, and simultaneously a deep compassion, connectedness, and goodwill for him or her arises in our heart. Similarly, spiritual love arising in the heart center can stimulate a corresponding "light-response" in the crown center. Thus "love-light" in the spiritual realm is the higher correspondence of "desire-mind" in the ordinary psyche-cylinder world.

Finally, unlike the forehead and solar plexus centers, which are wide open and through which we send our awareness and attention at will, our crown and heart centers are often only partially open, or even closed all together. (Naturally, our first goal in the PLS meditation will be to fully open them.)

We can summarize our ideas about the spiritual realm thus:

- The "spirit-funnel" represents the vertical, inward, background, spiritual realm of our being.
- The crown center is the door to our Self-Identity and higher nature.
- This door is open only partially or not at all in most people.
- Opening the crown-door (via properly-designed meditation) gains us entry to this realm.

D. Summary

If we stand back from the details of our model and consider the big picture, we see two different factors in operation and competing for our energy and attention. For lack of better terms, we could call these two factors "spiritual" and "worldly," and contrast their characteristics in the table on the facing page.

Further, we see that these two factors—higher and lower nature, Self and not-self—reside in specific realms, and that pathways and doors exist along which and through which we can send our attention into those realms.

Together, these two sets of facts create the possibility and desirability of meditation. The following chapters will explain what obstacles we will encounter in learning it, and how to do it.

	Spiritual Factor	**Worldly Factor**
Location	Background	Foreground
Orientation	Vertical, Inward	Horizontal, Outward
Center/Door	Crown & Heart	Forehead & Solar Plexus
Commingled Dualities	Light-Love	Desire-Mind
Identity	Self / Real "I"	Mask-Facade-Ego / False "I"
Attributes	Calm, quiet Motionless Simple Focused Energy-generating Direct seeing	Agitated, noisy Always in motion Complex Scattered Energy-depleting Derived ideas/concepts

13

THE NECESSITY FOR MEDITATION

A. Imagining Our Model in Motion

Our model depicting the human psyche represents only a snapshot of a system in constant motion. To understand why meditation is necessary and what it can (and must) accomplish, we need to be able to view and study this motion. Unless we happen to be clairvoyant, the only way we could do this objectively would be through a computer animation. But since none presently exists, we must use the only other means available—our subjective imagination. Only thus will we be able to picture the model in motion and observe what obstacles we face in trying to meditate, and how to offset them.

B. What Happens in Ordinary Living, and How, and Why

Continuous thinking

We must begin by picturing the model's mental "plane" as a sea of energy in ceaseless, restless motion, endlessly generating waves of thoughts (images, memories, concepts, ideas, etc.). As we interact with this realm by seizing on various ones of these thoughts, brooding over them, strengthening them, joining them with other thoughts and various feelings, etc., we add energy to the system and increase its motion. Thus by its own active nature and our equally active collaboration with it, our mind functions in effect as a perpetual thought-making machine.

So continuous and habitual is the resulting mental commotion and chaos and thought-creation that we regard it as normal. We think, "My mind is *supposed* to be in constant motion, always thinking, and I am *supposed* to go along with it and follow every thought wherever it leads." So we permit our attention to be pulled out toward, and captured by, the thought pyrotechnics before us. If we imagine our attention as a being—let us call it "attention-man"—we could picture it repeatedly yanked out to thought-forms and "Velcroed" onto them, then tossed to and fro like a sailor lashed to the mast of a ship. Most of us never imagine trying to break our captivity to these thought-forms by reining in our "attention-man" or silencing our mind by forcing it to stop moving.

So what happens as a result of this uncontrolled, unregulated thinking? First, we create a gazillion thought-forms, *which then become our possessions*. It is as if we went to a "mental Walmart," bought one of everything, and brought it all home to our "mental house" (mind). Now we are burdened with a ton of worthless stuff—we have an entire store's worth of mental objects crammed into the confines of our mind! And not only that, but imagine that every item we bought at a physical Walmart were alive and writhing around. That would describe the nightmare nature of this mass of living thought-forms in our mind, continuously enlarging, shrinking, changing shape and color and content, just like the images on a television screen.

Second, if we imagine our mind as a "mental muscle" and each thought as a flexing of that muscle, then our continuous thinking means that *our mind is always flexed and never relaxed*. As a result, it never has a chance to rest and rejuvenate itself through "mental sleep" (quiescence, motionlessness). The result is a perpetual state of mental tension, stress, and fatigue which reduces our ability to analyze, reason, deduce, discriminate, etc., at optimum capacity or efficiency. In simple terms, we cannot think clearly. Further, all that mental tension inevitably transfers itself into our physical head, face, and neck. (The next time you realize how "flexed" your mind is, observe the state of the muscles in your forehead, eyes, cheeks, lips, jaw, etc.)

Finally, continuous thinking (and feeling) means *continuous contact with the lower nature energies and not-self.* (Recall from our model that the mental and emotional realms are where they reside.) This, as we pointed out earlier in Chapter 2, works against our higher interest by creating habits that strengthen the lower nature:

> ...when [each] episode of mental activity ceases, another habit legacy remains: we have accustomed our mind to certain types of vibrations, and it learns to reproduce them easily and readily. Tendencies are thus born which, repeated often enough, become thought-habits—for good or ill —that are powerfully resistant to change. (p. 20)

> Every lower-nature energy that we permit to agitate [our "emotional body"]—irritation, criticism, anxiety, humorlessness—trains it to vibrate accordingly. When the agitation eventually ends, a vibratory legacy remains: like a robot, our emotional nature has been programmed, and remembers. (p. 18)

The illusion of horizontal knowing

It is a basic human instinct to seek to know, to learn, to figure things out. When thoughts arise in our mind, they naturally attract our attention, and we want to look at them, hear them, touch them, to see what they are about. In other words, we experience the mental equivalent of craving a physical sensation of some object. For example, our attention rushes out to read a billboard or remember a gossipy phone conversation or speculate about what X meant when she said Y. We think that by doing this, we will come to "know" something and gain satisfaction. Yet our model shows fundamental flaws in this notion.

As we pointed out in the previous chapter, all the thought-forms that arise in the mind are just that—artificial forms representing something else:

> ...when we think of a material object like a house or landscape, we construct a tiny image or replica of that object that we view with our inner eye; when we think of other people, we create miniature portraits of them. (p. 144)

Thus people, situations, circumstances—all are replicas, not the things themselves. The same is true of concepts, belief systems, memories, speculations, information imported via reading and studying, etc. The fact is that we do not know any of these things in themselves, but only the images of them that we create in our minds. Further, these image-objects themselves do not know anything, any more than a lamp or a chair or any other physical object knows anything. They are just mental energy-substance formed into temporary shapes and set into motion. Therefore they contain no knowledge that we can extract from them by touching or consulting them.

Understanding these two facts leads us inevitably to a third: that the very knowing that we crave exists not in the mind or any of its thought-creations, but in the Self/funnel. It is there and there alone that the light of recognition, intuition, and realization resides, and where our "inner light-bulb" flashes and our "ah-ha!"/insight moments occur. (Refer to the drawing on p. 147.) But our illusion impels us to continue directing our attention horizontally outward instead of vertically inward, seeking in vain in our mind and thoughts what is only within the Self.

The unvisited Self

Meanwhile, as we engage in all this continuous thinking and fruitless chasing after mental "knowing," the Self lies silently present in the background of our consciousness. Yet because we habitually direct our attention outward and not inward, we never contact this Self. No contact means that we go through life never really knowing our real Identity, but instead live in a state of confusing it with the not-self—the mass of thoughts, feelings, and physical sensations that overwhelms our attention and holds it captive. Fortunately, a way exists to escape this "Self-deluded" bondage if we are willing to employ it: meditation.

C. What Could Happen Through Meditation, and How, and Why

Restraint of the thought-making tendency of the mind

The two facts that we described in the previous section—the mind's continuous thinking and our own fruitless chasing after mental "knowing"—are simply part of the conditioning and functioning that nature has built in to minds and human beings. Yet once we determine that these activities do not serve our higher interest, we are free to oppose and offset them, just as we do when we brush our teeth or exercise our muscles to ward off natural decay or atrophy. In a similar fashion, it is quite possible to intervene to restrain our mind and arrest its natural motion. Viewing the model in our imagination, we can picture ourselves commanding the "thought-waves" on the mental "sea" to subside, and along with them the roar that their motion produces.

Creation of the quiet necessary to "hear" the Self

Once the mind's activity starts to lessen, a new situation arises in the relation between the still, calm Self and the restless, agitated mind. We can illustrate this development through a musical analogy. Imagine a full symphony orchestra of strings, winds, brass, and percussion. Let one instrument—an oboe, say—represent the Self, and all the other instruments represent the multitude of thoughts in the mind. When the full orchestra is playing, we cannot hear the oboe because its sound is drowned out by that of the other instruments. But let the conductor direct the other instruments to cease playing one by one until all fall silent, and eventually we will be able to hear every nuance of the oboe's notes.

Thus is the situation we face as meditators. The sole obstacle to hearing the Self is the noise in the mind produced by our many thoughts. Note that it is irrelevant what the thoughts are; or whether they are good or bad, pleasant or unpleasant, etc.; or why they may have arisen. It matters only to silence them by making the mind quiescent to be able to hear the Self. Note also that the quieter and less active our mind is when we begin to meditate, the easier it is to silence it. We can create this calmer initial state in two ways: by applying all the dispassion techniques we studied in Part I, which are designed to keep our mind, emotions, and nervous system unagitated; and by adopting a new attitude and ideal toward our mental functioning during the outward, non-meditating part of our daily lives:

- Eliminate unnecessary thinking and speaking; reduce the overall amount of both.
- Cease pursuing needless "knowledge"; know only what is necessary.
- Cultivate an aspiration to know the Self, and resolve to meditate regularly to accomplish this.

Redirection of our attention inward and "upward"

When the mind becomes quiescent and we can sense ("hear") the Self in the background, this frees us to reorient our attention. Whereas before we have let it be pulled outward through the forehead door toward the kaleidoscope of thought-forms in the mind, now we can imagine withdrawing it from this horizontal mental orgy and redirecting it inward toward the beckoning world of the Self. Through the open door in the center of the head, we can picture gazing "upwards" into this other world and bathing in the vertical downflow of the Self-energy.

Reception by the mind of the Self/higher nature light

Interestingly, the final event in this sequence of meditation effects returns us to the mind, where we began. But instead of actively creating its own thoughts as before, the mind now functions in an altogether different capacity: as a passive "photographic plate" on which are impressed the ideas, intuitions, insights, and understandings that flash forth from the Self-light and higher nature pouring in through the head center. No passage in the metaphysical literature captures the essence of this event as elegantly as this one that we quoted earlier in Chapter 2:

It is upon the serene and placid surface of the unruffled mind that the visions gathered from the invisible world find a representation in the visible one. It is with jealous care that we have to guard our mind-plane from all the adverse influences which daily arise in our passage through earth-life.—*Mahatma Letters*, 64.

In fact, we could say that the entire Personal Liberation System is contained in these two sentences: (1) the practice of meditation to render the mind quiescent (serene, unruffled) and to gather insights (visions) from the Self (invisible world), and (2) the practice of dispassion to guard our mind from the countless agitations (adverse influences) of life.

14

BEGINNING MEDITATION

A. The Basic Meditation Technique

Based on the ideas from the two previous chapters, we can define meditation as follows:

Meditation is that activity in which we deliberately (1) withdraw our attention from the not-self and lower-nature realm and (2) direct it to the Self and higher-nature realm, for some sustained period of time.

The outline on the facing page contains directions and suggestions for each part.

B. Commentary on the Outline

If we were learning an objective skill, say, tennis, we would begin with a set of instructions corresponding to the outline given. Then, as we stepped onto the court to attempt to play, we could have an instructor who could demonstrate the proper form for us or observe our movements and physically adjust them. But we can have no such instructor with a subjective skill like meditation. So from the point at which we try to put the instructions into practice, we are on our own and must teach ourselves through experiment and experience. As a partial substitute for the missing instructor, here is a collection of observations and suggestions that will help to focus and streamline your experiments, hasten the learning process, and address certain practical questions.

Meditation as a cumulative activity

Like the result of gaining strength from lifting weights, the desired result of meditation—the quieting of the mind and the attunement to the Self—happens gradually, not overnight. Each meditation session

> **PLS Beginning Meditation Outline**
> - **Withdraw your attention from the foreground of your consciousness.**
>   - Restrain the mind; impose motionlessness, stillness on its activity.
>   - Refuse to watch the foreground (thoughts, images, memories, etc.)
>   - Recall the idea that you do not need to know anything outward.
>   - Relax and luxuriate in not having to watch thoughts or think.
>   - Feel the freedom and lightness of having no mental possessions.
>   - If you lapse back into thinking, note how much effort/energy it takes.
>   - Ask yourself: Who am I apart from these thoughts? (Hint: the Self)
>   - Ask yourself: Is there any real reason to keep these thoughts? (Hint: no)
> - **Redirect your attention to the background of your consciousness.**
>   - Recall that the Self is located there and present at every moment.
>   - "Feel" to locate the head center; imagine it as an aperture or door.
>   - Imagine, and try to feel, the "vertical" stream entering through it.
>   - Listen for the Self—motionless, calm, thought-free, empowering.
>   - Repeat these actions each time you realize you've stopped doing them.
> - **Do these two parts simultaneously when possible, alternately when not.**
>   - Your attention will swing back and forth between the two poles.
>   - When you find yourself looking outward at your mind, withdraw your attention and feel for the background and head-center door.
>   - When you find yourself in the Self-stream, be attentive to what it takes to stay there.

adds to the accumulation of the new rhythm you are imposing on your mind and the opening of the pathway to the Self. The key to acquiring these accumulations is patient daily repetition. Without that, little of substance will happen.

Meeting the resistance of habits

When you first begin to meditate, you will naturally run head-on into your mind's habit of non-stop thinking. It may strongly resist your efforts to silence it, and you may be at a loss about how to proceed. Yet both these reactions are just what we would expect and no cause for alarm. It will help to recall the following principle of learning and act accordingly:

> Prior to experimenting, we cannot know or be able, so all learning must begin from blindness and inability. Our beginning actions are often difficult, awkward, inept, unsuccessful. While trying them, we often feel frustrated, uncomfortable, self-doubting, dispirited, hopeless. Such

feelings are misleading—they do not indicate that something is wrong, and they are not serious. Furthermore, paying attention to them actually retards the learning process. As long as we continue to act, even if blindly, our actions produce effects which accumulate, guiding us toward eventual knowing. (p. 82)

(In fact, you might find it useful to review all the learning principles, for example in the summary on p. 88.)

The role of effort

Like directing and focusing your eye, then letting images register on it, the PLS meditation is both active (restraining the mind, directing the attention) and passive (listening, feeling, receiving). Therefore, you must not try too much (headaches), but also not too little (no result). Perhaps the best description of the ideal balance is the phrase, "persistent slight effort." So during meditation, check periodically whether you have attained that balance, and adjust accordingly. In gauging adjustments, this passage from the previous chapter may help:

> ...if we imagine our mind as a "mental muscle" and each thought as a flexing of that muscle, then our continuous thinking means that *our mind is always flexed and never relaxed*. (p. 151)

Trying too hard (the more common imbalance) always results in a "flexed" or "clenched" mind. If you find yours so, simply imagine relaxing it in the same way that you relax a physical muscle (while keeping your attention directed toward the head center).

The importance of pairing dispassion with meditation

As you begin meditating regularly and reaping the benefits of a quiet mind and Self-communion, do not forget the crucial supporting role played by the practice of dispassion. Such a practice both safeguards the reservoir of higher energy accumulated during the previous meditation and preserves the mental and emotional quiet necessary for launching the next meditation. (To review this topic, refer to the Chapter 3 section *The Lower Nature Harms a Meditation Practice*, p. 21.)

The importance of directing and controlling thought

Along with practicing dispassion to avoid agitation, you can aid your meditation efforts by carefully monitoring and governing your thought throughout the day. During every moment, you choose where to direct your attention. As you do, train yourself to consider, "Is this topic of thought in my higher interest?" If not, intervene and make another choice. All the dispassion techniques we have studied employ some form of thought-direction, so if you are using them you are already doing this to some degree. Of these techniques, the last three presented—curbing unnecessary speculation, forgetting the past, and controlling speech—are particularly important ones for keeping the mind free of the kind of over-activity and clutter that is so inhospitable to meditation.

C. Physical & Practical Considerations

The physical environment

Two physical conditions are essential to meditation: solitude and silence. Choose a location where you can be alone. If you live with other people or restless animals, ensure that they will not intrude into your room while you are meditating. Turn off any electronic equipment or appliances emitting sounds that could hijack your attention. If your space suffers unavoidable noise intrusions from without (lawn mowers, barking dogs, city traffic, loud people, etc.), two items are indispensable. The first is a "white noise" sound machine (or CD or computer/phone app), which will mask many sounds that you cannot otherwise block out. The second is earplugs, a meditator's best friend. The most effective are the foam ones with a noise reduction rating (NRR) of 32 decibels or more. Finally, at the beginning at least, meditate with eyes closed to eliminate distractions of sight. (Later, you might find it an interesting experiment to try meditating with eyes open.)

Physical position and posture

The ultimate purpose of meditation is to solve the problem of false identification—the notion that you *are* your thoughts, feelings, and body, when your real identity and Self is none of those things. Thus the ideal physical position for meditating is one that removes your focus from your body and lets you forget that you have one. For example, choose a comfortable chair or couch that supports your back where you can sit upright, or make a similar set-up with pillows and a headboard on your bed. Arrange your legs however is most natural—cross-legged, knees drawn to chin, legs stretched out straight, feet on the floor, etc.—and change their position periodically as needed when doing long meditations. Avoid rigid, highly stylized "meditation positions" like the lotus position with outstretched arms and circled thumb/finger. Also avoid lying down: the body is simply too habituated to sleep in this position to make it appropriate for the increased alertness that meditation seeks.

Frequency

The ideal is to meditate twice daily: in the morning upon arising and again in the late afternoon (or, if not possible, then before bedtime). If you can fit only one session into your schedule, morning is the essential one.

Duration

If you have ever done yoga stretching, you know that (1) you must hold a pose for some minimum duration to produce any effect at all, and (2) the longer you hold it after that threshold, the greater the result. The same is true for meditation. You will probably find that the effective minimum is about twenty minutes, but that at least thirty minutes will produce a more satisfying result. After you get comfortable with whatever minimum you discover, experiment with pushing the time-envelope, since each additional minute adds to the new rhythm of quiet and inwardness. In my experience, something happens after thirty minutes that cannot happen earlier, no matter how skilled and experienced you are; and something else again after sixty minutes, and ninety, and 120. One experiment you can try is to break a long meditation into a string of shorter ones, for example:

20 min. + break + 20 min. + break + 20 min. = 1 hr. of meditation

Make the breaks about five minutes, and during them do something mindless like light housework or stretching. A scheme like this is highly effective: the effects accumulate, and the breaks actually improve the meditation. Another experiment is to try some long meditations (90-120 minutes) without a break to see what they are like.

The experience of time

The more active your mind, the slower time will seem to pass. At the beginning, when your mind is overly active, you can sit for what seems like thirty minutes, yet only five minutes will have passed. After you become more skilled, when your mind is deeply quiet and your head center is open, you will experience the reverse: what seems like five minutes will turn out to be thirty. The key is not to give up during the slow-time stage, as it is simply part of the passage to the faster-time one.

D. Frequently Asked Questions

What if my mind is so active that I can't even get past the first step?

For the moment, forget everything in the outline except "impose motionlessness on your mind." For example, pick an image that is in constant motion, and do not worry about trying to stop looking at it or to make it go away; just make it stop moving. Or, imagine that the cylinder wall before you is spinning around, and you are witnessing a kaleidoscope of images pass before you at high speed, as if you were on a rapidly spinning merry-go-round. Then extend your "inner hands" and press on the cylinder wall to slow and stop its motion by friction. Or invent your own imagery or method of restraining the motion. Whatever the method, once things stop moving, you will have liberated your attention from its captivity and can resume performing the rest of the actions in the outline.

Is practicing mindfulness in any way a part of the PLS meditation?

Mindfulness is described as the practice of focusing one's attention on the sensations, feelings, and thoughts occurring in the present moment. Observing these phenomena and establishing a keen awareness of them is obviously a useful practice. Indeed, the suggested exercises for each of the earlier PLS dispassion techniques invariably begin with "Identify when you are doing X..." or "Observe Y kind of thoughts...." So practice mindfulness whenever you find it helpful or necessary, but keep its limitations clearly in mind. First, it is not meditation as we defined it at the beginning of this chapter; it is merely the psychological equivalent of observing physical objects or physical events. Second, it is not an ultimate goal in itself, but only a means to the end of the Self dis-identifying with the not-self. Finally, if all you do is become aware of and observe your thoughts, nothing else happens: no active repudiation of needless thought and feeling, no withdrawal of attention from horizontal life, no attempt to open the head center, etc. It is like standing on a merry-go-round watching the scenery pass endlessly before you, instead of learning how to stop the merry-go-round and step off—and then doing so.

What about focusing my awareness on my breathing?

Your body and its sensations and functions constitute a major part of the not-self that you are trying to disentangle yourself from. Paying attention to your breath—or your elbow or lip or foot—merely makes you more aware of your body, whereas a goal of the PLS meditation is to enable you to forget that you have one. That said, if you find that measured breathing for a brief period helps to quiet your mind before you begin to meditate, there is no harm in doing it. Just be clear that focusing on the breath is not meditating.

I take it that guided meditation is not part of the PLS?

Correct. From the point of view of the PLS, the term "guided meditation" is an oxymoron. Based on our definition and the commentary on it, meditation is done inwardly, silently, and alone. But if a live or recorded voice is periodically speaking and instructing you to visualize this or affirm that or relax your body, in those moments your attention is pulled outward, the silence is broken, and you have company—which means that you are no longer meditating. To use the PLS meditation, the simple outline at the beginning of this chapter is the only guidance you need.

E. Beyond the Beginning Meditation

Over time, as we do the beginning meditation described in this chapter, the head center will open and reveal the hidden, background world of the Self. The contrast between this world and the ordinary, mundane one gives rise to a number of startling perceptions that radically remake our consciousness. Certain awarenesses dawn on us that become the seed of whole new levels and directions of meditation. The final two chapters describe the most important of these advanced topics and meditations. It is a good idea to read them as part of acquiring the big picture of the goals of the PLS, but to return to them later after the beginning meditation has produced its initial effects. For the more the head center is open and the Self-light registering, the more useful the ideas in these chapters will be.

15

Advanced Topic I
MIND AS A MOVIE THEATER

A. The Movie Analogy

Movies in the physical world

Imagine that it is the early twentieth century and that we have a friend, Louis, in the fledgling "motion picture" business who offers to give us a demonstration of this new and unfamiliar phenomenon. Louis first explains how these moving pictures are created, using the new terminology. A special camera takes multiple pictures each second of people or things in motion. The resulting pictures are printed in sequential "frames" on long strips of celluloid that have a series of evenly-spaced holes along either side. This "filmstrip" is then threaded into a second device, a "projector," whose sprockets align with the holes and grip the film. The sprockets turn and pull the frames of the film in front of a lamp, pausing and holding each frame there for a split second. During that instant, the light shines through the transparent celluloid, then through a lens on the other side that magnifies the images on the filmstrip and projects them out onto a screen. The sprockets then turn again, advancing to the next frame. During the transition between frames, a shutter blocks the light, and the screen goes momentarily black.

His explanation complete, Louis then escorts us into a darkened room where we will view one of his "movies." At that moment we are aware of ourselves in the room, as well as the room's various furnishings—a couch, chairs, lamps, a table with the projector on it, and a white screen on the wall before us. We seat ourselves, and Louis turns on the projector. Instantly, we feel our peripheral awareness shrink as our attention is drawn to the image of a crowded street—as yet unmoving—

that has suddenly appeared on the screen. For dramatic effect, Louis starts the film running at a very slow speed, so that we see the following sequence:

> still picture #1—black—still picture #2—black—still picture #3…

as if we were watching what we now call a slide show. At this point, we note that we are still clearly aware of ourselves seated in the room and the screen positioned a few feet away on which the images are projected, though not much else. Slowly but steadily, Louis increases the film speed, so that the interval between image and black screen shrinks and shrinks. Our eyes and brain still perceive the individual pictures and the spaces between them, but with increasing difficulty. Finally, the film speed crosses the threshold—about sixteen frames per second—above which we can no longer distinguish image from black, or one image from the next. [A video demonstrating this phenomenon and depicting the very scene described below is at www.thepls.org/resources/.]

Suddenly, astonishingly, as if conjured by magic, the bustling street scene leaps to life on the screen: horses and carriages, streetcars, throngs of pedestrians, all in motion exactly as in real life. Simultaneously, we feel our attention involuntarily sucked into the movie. We become engrossed in the setting and action and characters, to the point that we lose all sense of outer time and place. It is as if the screen had been a door through which our consciousness has passed into another world, one whose "reality" is so convincing as to supersede the physical world that we consider to be the real "real" one. During the time that the movie holds our attention captive, its characters are to us real people, its plot a series of events that are actually happening, its setting substantial streets and houses. It never occurs to us then that all these elements are merely tiny, inanimate shadows on frames of film sequentially presented to our vision at high speed so as to create a temporary, illusory universe. It is only later—when Louis stops the projector, the movie's entire world abruptly ceases to be, and our attention returns to physical "reality"—that we become aware of just how completely we had lost ourselves in the movie, and just how real it seemed while we were there.

The human psychological correspondence

The movie experience we have just described is a nearly exact correspondence to what happens in our own mind hundreds of times a day, and periodically during the night when we dream. The fact is that every one of us lives in a private, one-seat theater in which we experience a continuous series of interior movies that are created by us and known only to us. Before the advent of modern motion pictures in the 1890's, teachers and schools of thought used a range of analogies derived from nature to suggest this phenomenon. The Buddhist literature, for example, compares what happens in ordinary human consciousness to a dream, mirage, echo, apparition, magical creation, image in mirror, image of moon reflected in water, mock show, eye disease (eye floaters). The Indian sage Ramana Maharshi (born 1879) was the first teacher I know to employ the movie analogy. Let us investigate and develop his ideas so that we will recognize our experience of this "inner movie" phenomenon and understand how it happens. Then we will have a starting point for meditations that set us free from the bondage it imposes on us.

Ramana observed that the human psyche is actually a movie production studio and a movie theater all rolled into one. The production studio is the mind and its ability to create thoughts, ideas, concepts, memories, images, viewpoints, interpretations, etc. All these elements, in concert with our feeling nature, combine to form "thought stories" that become our inner movies. Like their outer counterparts, these inner movies have all manner of characters, settings, and plots, and are of every imaginable genre. A passage from the *Mahatma Letters* elegantly sums up this movie production capacity:

> Man is continually peopling his current in space with a world of his own, crowded with the offspring of his fancies, desires, impulses, and passions.

The viewing theater consists of an inner projector and a dual inner/outer screen. The lamp in this projector is the Self—recall the light bulb in our drawing, and our assertion that the light of understanding, insight, and awareness is located in the Self, not the mind. The filmstrip is the thought-stories described above. The motion inherent in all thought propels the "thought-story-filmstrip" forward, creating the movie. Both the "inner wall" of the "psyche-cylinder" and the outside world form the screen on which the movie is projected.

Once we have produced the elements of the movie in our thought and feeling, and the projector starts playing the movie, the same thing happens to our consciousness as it does when we watch outer movies. Our attention is sucked into the movie; we lose awareness of everything else, and forget that we have done so; and we are convinced for the moment that what we are experiencing is real, and not a movie.

B. The Science of Inner Movies

As accurate and intellectually helpful as this "inner movie" analogy may be, by itself it is unlikely to lead anyone to instant mastery (or even awareness) of this phenomenon. This is because most of us do not live primarily in our Self-center from where we can view our mind and emotional nature from a distance and with relative objectivity. So instead of seeing movies forming and playing in our psyche, we are blindly swept into them, oblivious to their existence and the effect they have on our perception. Even when we are operating from our center and can observe what is happening, the speed with which the movies form and our habit of rushing into them makes them difficult to resist. The only way to overcome these obstacles is through a close study of the science at work in every aspect of the inner movie process. Let us investigate.

Formation

In Chapter 13 we addressed the phenomenon of continuous thinking. We described how our mind creates thought-forms—mental "objects" composed of mental energy-substance—which are in constant motion. These thought-images attract our attention and pull it outward, where it "touches" the thoughts and "sticks" to them. We now need to add a crucial fact to that description: every one of those thought-forms that our attention latches onto is the mental equivalent of a television or movie screen. This is not, however, a fact that we realize when the screen first pops up. What we perceive in that initial split-second is a still, two-dimensional picture, like a painting hanging on a museum wall. It is only in the next split-second, when the image has captured our attention, that we discover that it is actually a *moving* picture—a movie playing on a screen. In the split-second after that, the screen becomes a door through which we pass into an apparently real, three-dimensional world created by the motion. In the final split-second, the door closes behind us, and whatever awareness of and link with our Self that we may have had the instant before, vanishes for the time being. We are now "in" the movie and subject to two powerful features of it which conspire to keep us there: its characters and situations, and the screen it is projected on.

Characters and situations

The characters are nearly always replicas of actual people outside us—parents, spouses, children, co-workers, friends, enemies, public figures, etc. Note that the same is often true of our dream-movies, except that those replica-characters often behave in ways so unlike their real-life counterparts that upon awaking, we rarely consider them to have been any sort of accurate representation of real people. Not so, however, with our waking movies. We tend to regard the replica-characters in them not as fictitious, but as identical to their outer counterparts. That is, we believe that the qualities, attitudes, viewpoints, motives, etc., which we attribute to these invented characters, exactly match the qualities, attitudes, viewpoints, motives, etc., possessed by their real outer counterparts. This false certainty perpetuates the forgetting that the movie has caused and reduces the likelihood of remembering and exiting.

The same phenomenon applies to our movies's settings and situations. They, too, are nearly always replicas of settings and situations outside us—personal relationships, school and office environments, social groups, family circumstances, financial conditions, etc. And as with our replica-characters, we routinely regard these invented replica-settings and replica-situations as identical to their outer counterparts and accurate presentations of them.

Projection

As we noted in the previous section, two screens exist: one within, the other without. Since dream-movies occur only when we are asleep, while they play we have no awareness of the outside world. Therefore they are projected onto only one screen, the one located entirely within the confines of our psyche. But our waking-movies are of an altogether different sort. They are projected both onto that screen within our psyche *and* simultaneously onto the screen that is the outside world. Further, these waking-movies frequently form in concert with our outer interactions. So, for example, as we have an exchange with a co-worker, we have an inner movie of that same exchange playing along with it. This movie naturally features the replica of the co-worker that we have created and is projected onto the actual co-worker in the outer world, so that the former is exactly superimposed on the latter. This even further cements our perception that we are experiencing one thing (the outside "reality") when actually we are experiencing another (an inner movie).

The resulting "world" and states of consciousness

These three factors—the movie forming and playing, the replica-characters and replica-situations it features, and its projection onto the outside world—create the world that we experience, live in, and regard as real in that moment. So if we dream that we are on a beach in the Carribean, our world in that moment is one of sun and surf and ocean vistas, not the darkness of the small room which we are sleeping in and oblivious of. Or if we are awake but lost in a thought-movie about financial ruin that could befall us and leave us living under a bridge in the freezing cold, then that movie is the world we live in for the moment, superseding the physical one in which we are seated in a comfortable chair in front of a warm fireplace.

In addition to conjuring the temporary worlds that we inhabit, movies also inevitably provoke the states of consciousness we experience while watching them. For example, if we dream that a man with a knife is chasing us and trying to kill us, our state of consciousness for that moment is panic, terror, desperation. It does not matter that in the physical world we are lying safely in a bed and in no danger whatever; the dream-movie state replaces what would otherwise be one of peace and contentment. Or, if we are awake and watching our favorite "reliving the past" freak-out movie—"Look at all the terrible choices I have made and am doomed to make again"—we easily fall into a state of pessimism, futility, and despair. It does not matter that already, in numerous instances, what we have learned from these past choices has enabled us not to repeat them; for the moment, the state of optimism and confidence that would accompany that fact is eclipsed by the opposite state arising from our lower-nature movie.

The outside world

Thus far, the only relation we have considered between the outer world and inner movies is that the former furnishes the models for the latter's replica characters and situations, and often serves as the screen on which they are projected. But there is another relation that is far more significant and can be startling to those who may have never realized it. Both Eastern philosophy and Western science point out that we have no direct knowledge of the outside world—whatever it may actually be—despite our certainty that we do. Instead, all we can know of it is a succession of images in our mind produced by the input from our five senses. Thus what we are actually experiencing when we perceive the external world is just another movie playing in our mind—a "five-senses-movie." And the world of this movie is no more "out there" than are the worlds conjured in the dream-movies and waking-movies previously described. Now this does not mean that there is no real outer world of people and houses and trees and cars. But it does mean that we are deluded when we believe that any "five-senses-movie" playing in our inner psyche *is* that external world, rather than an artificial and incomplete representation of it.

The unreality of all movies

When we first introduced the idea of the Self, we pointed out one of its main characteristics: "It is vividly and irrefutably *real*, and by contrast makes our thoughts, feelings, and the outer world seem dream-like and unreal." (p. 147) This brings us to the ultimate fact about movies from the point of view of the Self: the worlds that all of them create are not real, despite what we think while in them. Here is how Ramana describes it:

> [Both] the world of wakeful experience and the dream-world…are but creations of the mind. So long as the mind is engrossed in either, it finds itself unable to deny the reality of the dream-world while dreaming and of the waking world while awake. But if you withdraw your mind completely from the world and turn it within and abide thus—that is, if you keep awake always to the Self, which is the Substratum of all experience—you will find the world, of which alone you are now aware, just as unreal as the world in which you lived in your dream.—*Maharshi's Gospel, Books I & II*, 97–98.

And this essential unreality is a characteristic not just of our dream-movies and waking-movies, but equally of our five-senses-movie. Once we acknowledge this fact, many passages in the literature of Eastern philosophies about the world not being real—often a source of bewilderment and incredulity to Western readers—become more comprehensible. To its proponents, this idea is based on simple and impeccable logic: the world is a movie; movies are not real; therefore the world is not real. Here are some typical passages asserting this view:

> After all, what is objective life itself but a panorama of vivid unrealities?
> —*Mahatma Letters*, 103.

> For the [Knower of Self]…the world is no better than a repeatedly presented phenomenon of a dream.—*Maharshi's Gospel, Books I & II*, 124

> Apart from thoughts, there is no independent entity called the world. In deep sleep there are no thoughts, and there is no world. In the states

of waking and dream, there are thoughts, and there is a world also. Just as the spider emits the thread (of the web) out of itself and again withdraws it into itself, likewise the mind projects the world out of itself and again resolves it into itself. When the mind comes out of the Self, the world appears. Therefore, when the world appears (to be real), the Self does not appear; and when the Self appears (shines) the world does not appear. When one persistently inquires into the nature of the mind, the mind will end, leaving the Self (as the residue).—Ramana Maharshi, *Who Am I? (Nan Yar?)*, 4.

C. Problems Inherent in Inner Movies

Now that we understand something of the workings of inner movies, let us address the main problems associated with them.

Mismatches between movie characters/situations and actual ones

Needless to say, the combination of (1) letting our attention be sucked away from the Self and into a movie; (2) inventing replicas of people and situations, and attributing to those replicas qualities which they may or may not possess; and then (3) projecting the resulting movie onto the actual person or situation, is a recipe for delusion and disaster. Perhaps nowhere does this cause more problems than in our close personal relationships. In them, it is so easy to imagine that we are having a relationship with the actual other person, when instead it is with our self-created, inner-movie version of that person—often an altogether different being. Not only that, but our movie version of the person tends to block out any accurate perception of the actual person, even when he or she is plainly stating or demonstrating facts for all to see. This prevents us from using those facts to adjust our movie-replica-person to match the real one. It also often makes us the last to know what was apparent from the beginning to all our friends, who had no such inner movie interfering with their registration of the facts.

Movie mismatches inevitably cause misunderstandings, conflicts, pain, and suffering, both to ourselves and others. We create unrealistic expectations of others based on our false replica of them, and they suffer the discomfort and annoyance of trying to relate authentically with us while competing with an inauthentic version of themselves playing in our movie. Here is one PLS user's experience of the latter situation, as related in a recent consultation:

This is what I run into with ———— . He'll call me to discuss some matter concerning our son, for example, and I'll respond to something he says, and he'll say, "Whoa, wait a minute, I didn't mean for you to think that!" And I'm going, "You don't know what I'm thinking! What are you talking about?" He jumps the gun because his movie of me is playing and he isn't really hearing the actual me; he's just running whatever I'm saying through his "circuitry." And not only that, he seems to think that I'm somehow in his head—his movie—with him. It kind of makes me want to poke his eyes out with a pencil! {Laughing}

One reason it drives me crazy is that it's so inefficient. I have to (1) listen to what he thinks my reality is, (2) advise him that that is not in fact my reality, (3) listen to him protest, "Yes, it is too your reality," (4) advise him again that it isn't, then (5) *finally* get his movie adjusted so that we can address the matter he called about. It has gotten so bad that I don't even answer the phone when he calls unless I know I have twice as much time as I would need with a regular person who has no movie about me.

Mis-identification of problems

As long as we are deluded into thinking that the movie-worlds we enter are real, we also think that the problems contained in those movies are real. This in turn propels our attention even more deeply into the movie, for we are convinced that only by wrestling with the movie's problems can we solve them. Thus entangled and deceived, we do not realize that the actual problem is the movie itself—that it exists and that we are in it—and that the solution is to stop watching it and turn it off.

This fact is easy to see in the case of dream-movies. Consider, for instance, our earlier example of a dream in which a man with a knife is chasing us and trying to kill us. While lost in the dream, we are convinced that our problem is the man, the knife, and the threat to our life; and that the solution is to call the police or escape or shoot our pursuer. All this time, however, the real problem is that we are dreaming, and the real solution is to wake up. The instant we do, the dream-movie ceases to be, and along with it all the so-called "problems" it contained and the painful states of consciousness that accompanied them.

This fact is harder to discern or believe where waking-movies are concerned because, as we have seen, they are often playing simultaneously with outer situations or events, and are superimposed on them. Thus we confuse the two, creating a double whammy: not only do we mistake the problems in the movie for something real, but we are convinced that they exist outside us and are forced upon us. Yet the principle here is the same as in dreams, for, as Ramana points out,

> Waking is long and a dream is short; other than this there is no difference. Just as waking happenings seem real while awake, so do those in a dream while dreaming....—Ramana Maharshi, *Who Am I?*, 7.

Thus the real waking-movie problem is the unreal movie itself, not its contents; and the real solution is to "wake up," which annihilates both the movie and the troubles it contains. But "waking up" from a waking-movie is not so simple or natural as waking up from a dream. It requires awareness of the Self gained through meditation, coupled with a willingness to adopt a radical new attitude toward each movie: that it knows nothing and is not about anything but itself, and that the "problems" it presents are phantoms requiring no effort on our part to solve. Instead, we must redirect all our resources toward simply withdrawing from it.

Forgetting

In general, the whole problem of forgetting is *the* problem of earth life. It is a fiendish trap, for by definition, "to forget" is not only "not to remember," but "not to remember that we have forgotten." And no phenomenon is more perfectly constituted to promote forgetting than inner movies. First, their very nature—the hypnotic convincingness, the apparent reality of the worlds they conjure—causes us to forget that we are even in one. Just as it would be difficult to graduate from a school if we did not even know we were attending one, so is it difficult to "graduate" out of movies when to do so we must remember that they will lure us into forgetfulness, but then forget that fact the moment we are thus lured. Second, while they hold us captive, nothing more thoroughly severs every link with and awareness of the Self and its world. Again, only meditation can finally deliver us from this "forgetting trap," through opening our head center and establishing a permanent anchor point for the Self. The latter then serves as an "anti-forgetting" outpost, always present and accessible in the back of our consciousness, no matter how deeply we become entangled in movie-world and forget.

D. Meditation for Disentangling from Inner Movies

The meditation for freeing ourselves from the bondage of inner movies is a tweaked version of the basic meditation from Chapter 14, using the passages below as a guide:

> When the mind…becomes quiescent [i.e., motionless–SR], the world will disappear.—Ramana Maharshi, *Who Am I? (Nan Yar?)*, 4.

The process of meditation is to remove the world from the mind. When the world subsides from the mind, even for a short time, it brings two things: (1) knowledge of the truth [the Self–SR] in degrees and (2) dispassion for the unreal world [the movie–SR].—Baba Hari Dass, *Talks: Knowledge and Dispassion*. www.mountmadonna.org/yoga/talks/twb9610.html

When the world, which is what-is-seen, has been removed, there will be realization of the Self, which is the seer.—Ramana Maharshi, *Who Am I? (Nan Yar?)*, 3.

…the realization of the Self, which is the substrate, will not be gained unless the belief that the world is real is removed.—Ramana Maharshi, *Who Am I? (Nan Yar?)*, 3.

Here is the meditation:

PLS Meditation for Disentangling from Inner Movies

- Recall the primary facts about inner movies.
  - They arise and capture your attention without your realizing it.
  - They are mental pictures in motion.
  - They create whatever world you inhabit in a given moment.
  - That world seems real, but is not.
  - That unreal world eclipses the real world of the Self.
  - Meditation can reveal these facts directly to you.
- Define the meditation's purpose: remove the world from your mind.
- Turn your attention inward and survey your psyche.
  - Identify any movie playing in it.
  - Note that the world created by the movie is not real.
  - Note that stilling your mind will make this unreal world vanish.
- Make the moving pictures stop moving by an act of will.
  - The pictures then remain, but now they are still.
  - Your attention is still directed to the screen, watching them.
- Withdraw your attention from the pictures and the screen.
- Let it "float" backwards into the region of your head center.
- Look "upward" and feel for the Self and its world of reality.
- When you register Self-light, pictures & movies temporarily vanish.
- Note the contrast between the real Self-world & unreal movie-world.
- When your attention is drawn outward again, movies will resume.
- Repeat the meditation steps each time this happens
- Your skill will increase with each meditation session.

In addition to the outline above, two other items may be of use in applying this chapter's ideas. First, here are thoughts and suggestions (in no particular order) about inner movies that you can apply when you are meditating and when you are going about your outer daily life:

- Check yourself regularly for whether you are in a movie.
- Be attentive to mismatches between your movie-replicas and actual people and situations. When you discover one, correct it.
- Remember: movies are not about anything except themselves, even when their characters and situations are replicas of those outside us.
- It is OK to relax and stop watching movies and not take them seriously and not believe anything they say.
- Movies determine our moment-by-moment consciousness.
- Each day we make thousands of small but momentous choices of what to identify with. These choices determine the subjects of our thought life and where our attention goes. By choosing wisely, we can avoid hours, days, weeks, months, years of bad movies and the needless stress, pain, and suffering that accompany them.

Second, below is a reproduction of an index card that I made for myself and consulted daily during a period of long meditations to study the phenomenon of inner movies. I found that it summarized the essential ideas and kept my attention focused on realizing and applying them.

Inner-Movie Meditation Reminders

The background Self is contacted vertically through the head center.
The foreground world is contacted horizontally through the ajna center.

The process of meditation is to remove the world from the mind.
When the world (what-is-seen) is removed, one will realize the Self (seer).

When the mind comes out of the Self, the world appears (as a movie).
When the mind becomes quiescent, the world-movie will disappear.

Apart from thoughts, there is no independent entity called the world.
The mind invents everything; if you see this, all vanishes & YOU remain.

Is there no difference between waking and dreaming?
Waking is long, a dream is short; other than this there is no difference (both are movies).

Realizing the Self requires removing the belief that the world is real (i.e., not a movie).
Realizing the Self is not possible while the world is taken as real.

16

Advanced Topic II
MIND AS A CONCEPT CREATOR

Thus far in the meditation chapters we have focused on the still mental images that we called thought-forms and the inner movies that form when they are in motion. Now we must shift our attention away from these "mind-forms" and direct it to the formless world of abstract concepts. As usual, we will seek to answer the essential PLS questions about this world: What are concepts and how do they behave? How do they hold us in bondage? How we can free ourselves from this limitation through meditation?

A. The Science of Concepts

Types of concepts

Simply put, concepts are ideas or notions that we create about ourselves, the world, and the relation between them. Concepts come in many varieties. Perhaps the most basic type is names we create for tangible objects: tree, car, table, star, ball. While such objects clearly exist in the physical world, our names for them and the ideas we associate with them constitute a separate, parallel world from the physical one. For example, our mental concept of "tree" is a different entity from any particular physical oak or pine, as is our concept of "money" from physical coins or bills.

A second type is labels or categories that we invent for roles that we play, like mother, son, boss, teacher, or host. Again, though these roles may have a physical existence, in our minds we have a world of counterparts of them consisting of our ideas of what a mother or boss or teacher is or should be.

A third type is names of intangible qualities or characteristics that we observe about humans and human life: agility, possessiveness, justice, failure, freedom, intelligence, time. Concepts of this kind are more purely abstractions than the previous two types, as they neither arise directly from our physical senses nor exist as mental images or pictures. Yet despite being formless, they create a mental world that exists independently of, and unknown to, the physical one we perceive when awake. Nature, for instance, knows nothing of calendars or clocks; but to us, who conceive of time and duration, "Thursday" and "April" and "4:00 p.m." are real phenomena in our private mental world.

A fourth type is more complex concepts that originate from our capacity to reason and draw conclusions from observation and experience. It is here that we find those concepts of most interest and relevance to the PLS: beliefs, assumptions, interpretations, impressions, opinions, meanings, views, convictions, judgments, theories, creeds, ideals, etc. Also in this group are topics that we investigated in Part I of this book, like expectations, seriousness, mistakes, and speculations. Here are a few examples of the many varieties of this concept type, as we might express them in words:

- I am a person forever doomed to bad luck in relationships.
- I regard her as a friend.
- Surely Sam didn't mean what he said.
- Whatever happens is what is supposed to happen.
- Janice will probably hate me after what I said.
- I can't go out looking like this.
- I have made a terrible mistake.
- I believe that age is irrelevant.
- My philosophy centers around reincarnation and karma.
- I assume that the teacher knows what she's talking about.
- I'd never do that to her, so surely she wouldn't do it to me.

Like names and labels, the concepts in this category create an independent inner world which we experience simultaneously with the physical one. Significantly, this particular concept-world interacts extensively with our inner-movie-world: our notions and ideas spawn movies that depict them, and the movies we watch give rise to conceptions about their meaning, significance, and "reality." So, for example, a belief that we are doomed in relationships may provoke movies in which we suffer rejection and unhappiness; and images of ourselves as an unattractive and flawed partner may create or strengthen the belief that we are cursed in romance.

Finally, we should note that while concepts of all these four types are a purely mental phenomenon, they often provoke and become closely associated with feelings and emotions in varying degrees. Naturally, simple name-concepts like "desk" or "house" tend to elicit fewer and milder feelings (if any) than a passionately-held belief or opinion. Our experience of concepts of this latter kind is usually of a hybrid "thought-emotion," in which the feeling component is initially the more visible and "tasteable," like the chocolate part of a chocolate-covered peanut. But we may be sure that like the peanut, some mental notion or belief or ideal is always present at the core when we "bite into" it.

Clusters of concept

Naturally, individual concepts do not exist in isolation, but join and merge with other related ones to form what we could call "concepts clusters." For example, ideas about tradition, respectability, propriety, security, safety, conformity, normalcy, rules, social obligations, etc., all contribute to the concept cluster named "conventionality." Similarly, our beliefs about who we are, what appearance we must present to society to succeed, what others expect of us if they are to accept us, what we ought to or must hide about ourselves from others, and countless other such notions, form the concept cluster that is the facade or persona (Latin, *mask*) that we present to the world. Of course there are countless other examples, but these two happen to be of particular interest to the PLS because of their imprisoning nature.

All concept clusters produce the same effects as individual concepts—create an inner world separate from the physical, form a lens through which we view situations and people, provoke various emotional responses—but these effects are even more pronounced and extensive due to their multiple components.

Sources of concepts

All the concepts that exist in our mind arise from one of two sources. The first is obviously ourselves: we think, reason, speculate, interpret, react to feelings, philosophize, etc., and form concepts based on these actions. In theory at least, it is possible for us to do this conceptualizing alone and independently, uninfluenced by anything outside ourselves. The second is other people, who use their creative power to do the same thing we do: think, reason, etc., and thereby form concepts. These concepts can range from the intensely personal, to ideas about relationships, education, society, politics, culture, to belief systems like religion and philosophy. We encounter these other-created concepts via various avenues—speech, books, magazines, radio, television, the internet, etc.—and import them into our minds and adopt them as our own. In practice, of course, self-created concepts and imported ones mix and blend and influence each other, so that our concept-world is an amalgam of the two sources. And for many (if not most) people, the bulk of their concept-world is composed of imported ideas, not ones that they have thought out for themselves.

Given this widespread importing of concepts from without, we need to note a crucial fact about the mass of thoughts created by humanity as a whole. In Chapter 13, we saw that in the PLS model, thoughts are mental objects ("thought-forms") that, once created by any thinker, have an independent existence and float around in the atmosphere. When we consider all the souls currently alive and thinking, and all the departed ones who have left behind their thought-legacy, we realize the staggering number of thought-forms that inhabit the world. Thus just as we live surrounded by an ocean of air pressing on our body from all sides, so also do we live in an ocean of concepts that presses relentlessly on our mind. And just as we are unconscious of the physical atmosphere and the pressure it exerts, so are we equally unconscious of the mental atmosphere and its pressure, and of the plethora of ideas reflecting our society, culture, and nation that stealthily enter our mind. Here is how one PLS user described her experience of this "unconsciousness factor" in a recent conversation about conventionality:

> I think of myself as a decidedly unconventional person, and I'm pretty sure most other people agree that I am. But nearly every day I am surprised to find some conventional concepts in my mind that have entered from who knows where. [Mimics her thoughts] "*I* can't write a four-letter word on Facebook! [*concept*] That would be nasty-talk! [*concept*] My students might think badly of me. [*concept*] They might quit my classes. [*concept*] My poor father would turn over in his grave." [*concept*] Or, "I can't let my son know about this or that thing going on in my life. [*concept*] That's not something a *son* should know." [*concept*] [Laughing] Uh, who says? Well, obviously, conventional concepts that have infiltrated my mind, that's who says—even as I think of myself as free of such things. I catch myself at this *every day*! And I'll tell you what else: if someone claims they don't have the same thing going on, they are probably a big fat liar. [Laughter] Because it's everywhere. It's in the air. You can't get away from it. It presses on you and seeps into your mind.

Projection of concepts

As soon as we create or import various concepts and concept clusters, and establish them as mental possessions, they begin to project themselves onto the outer world. In the previous chapter we studied the projection phenomenon as it relates to inner movies; the same principles and processes we found there apply equally to concepts. Each concept forms a lens through which we view the world. When we look through this lens, we see the concept projected and superimposed onto people and situations, causing them to appear a certain way. We then mistakenly regard this appearance as "the way things are," when actually it is "the way our concepts are." Suppose, for instance, that we have the concept that people are to be feared. When we encounter someone, instead of seeing simply "Person," we see "Frightening Person," since we view him through this fear lens or preconception. Furthermore, we are convinced by our projection that the "frightening-ness" of the person is an energy in him that he is radiating toward us. Ironically, of course, it is really the other way around: it is *we* who possess the energy and *we* who are doing the radiating! And what is more, we are routinely oblivious of this fact—a sobering testament to projection's limitless deluding power.

Conditioning by concepts

Once concepts are in place and projected, and we have fallen into believing the appearance they produce, they begin to condition our consciousness. Our thoughts and feelings fall into line with the particular notions or viewpoints or assumptions, and, like water running down a hill, they soon carve out a channel in which they all tend to flow from then on. In this way it becomes more or less automatic for us to think and feel along certain lines, and exclude all others.

Suppose, for example, that we import major parts of the conventionality concept cluster mentioned earlier. As a result, this cluster conditions our outlook about a broad swath of life—relationships, marriage, parenting, education, finances, careers, etc. Our thoughts and feelings about all these aspects follow accordingly, so that their character becomes established as traditional, conformist, orthodox, unquestioning, subservient, etc. Eventually we have no thoughts or feelings that are outside the "conventionality box"—they simply never occur to us, or if we hear about them from others, they either make no impression on us or provoke so great a resistance as to prevent our considering or exploring them. Thus do we arrive at the end of this process thoroughly conditioned by the conventionality concept-cluster. Naturally, all the concepts we allow into our mind set into motion this same process.

Subtlety of concepts

Unlike inner movies, which we can plainly see and hear, concepts are formless and invisible to our mind's eye. This renders them subtle, elusive, and difficult to maintain a clear awareness of as they expand into every corner of our psyche. Their effect on our perception is akin to sunglasses that we put on and forget we are wearing, so that we are unaware of both their presence and the coloring they project onto what we see.

Before we move on to the problems that concepts create, we might note that with the introduction of the world of concepts, we now have four "worlds" to be aware of as we apply the various PLS methods:

1. The (form) world reported by our five senses
2. The (form) world created by our inner movies
3. The (formless) world created by concepts
4. The (formless) world of the Self

We might also recall that from the Self's viewpoint—the one that all the PLS meditations are designed to help us attain—the first three are artificial, ever-changing, and therefore unreal worlds that we *perceive*; whereas the fourth is unchanging, vividly and irrefutably real, and who we really *are*.

B. Problems Inherent in Concepts

Many problems caused by concepts are identical to the ones we identified when considering thought-forms and inner movies. First, despite their formless nature, concepts function as mental objects. As such, they have a weight that is burdensome to carry around, which is probably the first thing people notice when they escape some particularly oppressive notion or mind-set ("I feel like a huge weight has been lifted off me!"). Also as such, they clutter our mind; again, we notice this keenly when we jettison a concept cluster and suddenly experience how much more spacious and simplified our thinking is. Second, concepts pull our attention horizontally outward toward themselves and all the thoughts and feelings they spawn. This cuts off our access to our head center, and through it our reception of the vertical energy stream containing our Self and higher nature. Finally, concepts create an unreal world and hypnotize us into believing it and the "problems" in it. Yet just as inner-movie worlds are not real, neither are concept worlds and their supposed problems. But if we do not understand the science involved, we are convinced otherwise, and we spend endless time and energy on "solutions" that ultimately do not work.

Beyond these problems lies another, perhaps the most fundamental of all: every concept gives birth to a limit or restriction or barrier of some kind. Conventional concepts limit our thought and actions to what society or our peer group considers respectable, secure, safe, "normal." Our mask limits us to showing only a small part of our self, or showing a "self" that is wholly unlike our real one. A conviction that we are cursed in relationships erects barriers to establishing and functioning in one. A prejudice or preconception about people restricts our ability to see who they actually are. An assumption that we could never accomplish something stops us from trying it. A rigid adherence to a given school of thought or belief system prevents us from considering other viewpoints about life and the world. Whatever the particular concept, in some way or other it establishes an artificial frontier or boundary beyond which our thoughts and actions may not pass. This creates two major problems that are among the most painful that humans experience.

The first is that all these limitations act as authorities and controllers, and like sheep we submit to them and become enslaved by them. The effect is bondage and the suffering and constriction of life's possibilities that follow from it. Here is how one PLS user described her experience:

> I was thinking back on how miserable it was to be conventional and live behind a facade, being careful what you say and do and abiding by expectations that others may have for you. I remember the "concept fog" I used to live in and how it limited my spiritual life, what I chose to read, who my friends were, what experiments I could try, and my creativity. As a result, for such a long time, I lost my true identity, who I really, really *am*.

When we analyze our incarceration by concepts, we find both good news and bad. The good news is that the "concept-prison" that holds us is illusory: its bars and locks are composed not of tempered steel, but only of ethereal ideas—mere abstractions. As such, this "prison" has no more real power to confine anyone than the one pictured on the front of my favorite birthday card (reproduced by the kind permission of the American Greeting Corporation, ©AGC, LLC):

THE MORON MAXIMUM SECURITY PENITENTIARY

Just as these "inmates" can step over the physical picket fence and walk past their "guards" at any moment, so can we do the same in our psyche with their mental counterparts. To do that, however, we must first realize that we are in prison and that escape from it is desirable and possible—and that is where the bad news comes in. For as we noted above, concepts have tremendous deluding power not only (1) to convince us that the view seen through their lens is the normal, unchangeable "way things are," but also (2) to make us forget (or never know) that we are looking through a lens at all! When this happens, we do not even register the fact that we are in bondage, much less how and why. We are then like the oblivious inmates on the back of the same card [top of facing page]. Needless to say, we must devise a way to avoid or awaken from this oblivion and bondage if we are to fulfill the exhortation written inside the card:

IT'S YER BIRTHDAY—BE FREE!

This brings us to the second problem: even when through meditation we succeed in accessing the Self and the powerful "freedom-concepts" in its world, we often find ourselves unable to act on them because of the fierce opposition of all the limiting concepts that populate our mind. An example that we used in Chapter 2 illustrates this problem:

> A woman registers intuitively that her present relationship is unhealthy and not in her or her partner's best interest. When she imagines ending it, she feels free, joyous, unburdened, and back on the right track. Simultaneously, she feels terrified of being alone, full of self-doubt that she is lovable, and worried that she will be unable to find a place to live and support herself. (p. 13)

Note that the precipitating factor in all the woman's burdensome, lower reactions is limiting concepts: "I can't be alone. I'm not loveable. I won't be able to find an apartment or job." By contrast, all her intuitive realizations are liberating Self-concepts: "This relationship is unhealthy. It's in no one's higher interest. Ending it would put me back on the right track."

The woman would of course like to act on the higher ideas and experience the lightness and freedom that they promise. In theory, this should be easy: the instant the Self-concepts registered in her head, she would incorporate them into her thinking and act on them. But in practice, when she transfers these "freedom-concepts" into her mind, they collide with the cluster of imprisoning concepts that she has created or imported. As a result, she finds herself caught between irreconcilable pairs of opposites, wanting and trying to follow what she knows is the better choice, but meeting opposition at every moment from her "concept-jailers." And of course this conflict and paralysis are inevitably accompanied by stress, torment, pain, suffering, etc.—a fact no doubt familiar to every reader.

C. Solving the Concept Problem: Analysis & Meditation

It should be clear from the foregoing analysis that rearranging concepts, or trading one set for another, or trying to work around them, is not going to solve the problems they cause; the only real solution is to eliminate them altogether. This may seem like a radical idea—living without beliefs, interpretations, assumptions, categories, labels, roles, etc.—yet for centuries this has been a primary goal in the best meditation schools and teachings. The Buddhist literature, for example, describes it as "having no notion or non-notion at all"; Ramana Maharshi called it "remaining without concepts." Let us adopt these prescriptions as our starting point, analyze how to incorporate them into our thinking, and create a meditation to accomplish the actual "concept-subtraction."

Analysis

For our analysis, let us use a familiar, representative concept as an example. For this purpose, we will choose beliefs, and consider two questions about them: How is it possible to "have no beliefs or non-beliefs" and "remain without beliefs"? And why is it in our higher interest to do so? Our first clue lies in a typical dictionary definition:

Belief: an acceptance that a statement is true or that something exists.

Note that the definition is not "knowledge that a statement is true or that something exists." If we know, we do not use the word *believe*. We do not, for instance, say, "I believe the traffic light is red" when we are sitting at an intersection looking up at it. Conversely, when we do use *believe*, it is precisely because we do not know. Beliefs—and convictions, interpretations, opinions, assumptions, etc.—are not facts or knowledge, however strongly we may feel or assert that they are. Once we admit and accept this, then inventing and adopting a belief about a person, thing, or situation does not really make much sense: not only does it not change the facts or reveal what they are, but it saddles us with all the problems we listed above.

As usual in the PLS, the method for breaking the habit of adopting beliefs begins with activating our imagination. In this case, we must imagine how we could live perfectly well without the belief, and imagine how doing so would improve our life. Fortunately, we need look no further than the mind of a scientist for an example of this technique at work. A real scientist lives in a perpetual state of "remaining without beliefs." In their place, he has hypotheses which he seeks opportunities to test. If he has such opportunities and can conduct such tests, he has knowledge based on the results. But as long as he is unable to test his hypotheses, he refrains from inventing beliefs based on wishful thinking, idealism, conventional ideas, doctrines imported from some school of thought, personal prejudices, personal desires, etc. Instead, he is perfectly willing not to know for the time being—obviously a practical attitude, since the facts are that at that moment he cannot and does not know.

This attitude of refusing to invent belief-concepts immunizes the scientist against every problem that we identified in the previous section. His mind is not cluttered with a mass of beliefs that take up space and weigh him down. He has nothing to defend, argue about, or refute attacks on. He has no beliefs that he hopes or wishes are true, or that cause him to suffer disillusionment and despair if they turn out to be untrue. No beliefs provoke lower-nature reactions that cloud his thinking and drain his energy. No artificial "belief-world" arises to color his view or swallow his identity. Perhaps most importantly, no beliefs pull his attention outward, so he is free to direct it inward (i.e., meditate) to the place where the creative flashes of intuition that furnish his hypotheses and fuel his experiments originate. Finally, when a new insight challenges one of these hypotheses, no imprisoning beliefs exist to resist it or oppose changes to it, and he suffers no pain or conflict or torment from altering or discarding it. All these effects leave the scientist free to be a scientist and enjoy a rich and satisfying scientific life.

Meditation

Now that we see how "remaining without beliefs" can be incorporated into our thinking, we can apply the same analysis and imagination to all our other concepts. Following is a tweaked version of the basic meditation to help us do this and thus subtract this major obstacle to finding and registering the Self. Since the meditation is designed to attack specific concepts, here is a reminder list of the various types mentioned throughout the chapter:

- *Concepts*—names, labels, categories, roles, beliefs, assumptions, interpretations, convictions, opinions, conclusions, judgments, theories, ideals, expectations, seriousness, mistakes, speculations
- *Concept-clusters*—conventionality (tradition, respectability, propriety, security, safety, conformity, normalcy, rules, social obligations) and our outer facade or mask (beliefs about who we are, what appearance

we must present to the world, what others expect of us if they are to accept us, what about ourselves we must hide from others, etc.)

PLS Meditation for Removing Concepts

- Define the meditation's purpose: remove the world from your mind.
- Direct your attention to your mind and choose a concept to address.
  - Note that the world created by this Concept X seems real, but isn't.
  - Note that removing Concept X will make the unreal world vanish.
- Imagine the possibility that you do not have to have Concept X.
  - Ask: Is Concept X necessary about this person/thing/situation/life?
  - Ask: What if I just stopped adopting Concept X about him/her/it?
  - Imagine "having no X or non-X" and "remaining without X."
  - Imagine the benefits: less clutter; no concepts to defend; nothing to cause disillusionment; no deluded views of life; no imprisonment.
  - Imagine how you would feel lighter, freer, less limited.
- Simultaneously with imagining, direct your attention inward.
  - Let it "float" backwards into the region of your head center.
  - Look "upward" and feel for the Self and its world of reality.
  - Note the contrast: real Self-world vs. unreal concept-world.
- Rest in the Self-light and note its effects.
  - It causes worldly concepts temporarily to vanish.
  - It replaces them with liberating "Self-concepts" from another world.
  - Through meditation you create the needed receptivity to them.
  - You need not struggle to create any concepts of your own.
  - You merely receive the ones inherent in the Self & its realm.
- Paraphrased ideas of Ramana Maharshi about the process.
  - Meditation goal: to not give room for even a single mental concept.
  - "Dwelling in solitude": state of freedom from mental concepts.
  - Bliss: experience of joy in state of "remaining without concepts."

D. The I-Thought

One concept stands apart from all the others and merits a section all its own: the I-thought. The I-thought is exactly what its name implies, a concept that we create of a personal self or ego (*Ego* is Latin "I"). This is, of course, an altogether different "I" from the enduring one which we have named the Self. The latter is our true identity or individuality, existing independently of, and unaffected by, our thoughts, feelings, and body, or anything in the outer world. The personal self created by the I-thought is the opposite: it is an impermanent, unreal "self" based on ever-shifting factors like our age, physical appearance, experiences, relationships, memories, social standing, education, successes and failures, beliefs, ideals, etc. Although it masquerades as a real "I," as a concept it is merely another mental construction and part of the non-self that we seek to disentangle ourselves from and deconstruct through meditation.

Any analysis of the bondage caused by concepts and the method of liberation from them leads inevitably to a fundamental fact about the I-thought: it is the one concept on which all the others depend for their existence. Ramana describes this phenomenon in grammatical terms:

> Of all the thoughts that arise in the mind, the "I" thought is the first. It is only after the rise of this that the other thoughts arise. It is after the appearance of the first personal pronoun [I] that the second and third personal pronouns [you, he, she, it, they] appear; without the first personal pronoun there will not be the second and third.—Ramana Maharshi, *Who Am I?*, 4.

To illustrate this principle, let us take as an example the (unhappy) idea, "I am a worthless loser." At first glance this appears to be a single concept. Yet it is actually two—"I" and "worthless loser"—which combine to create an unreal personal self or identity distinguished by a certain characteristic. In this way it is the psychological equivalent of a scarecrow, with the I-thought as its "skeleton" and the "worthless loser" concept as the clothing hung on it. As long as the I-thought skeleton remains intact, it can support an ever-changing wardrobe of limiting concepts, unreal inner movies, illusory thoughts, and lower nature feelings that make this inner scarecrow seem like a real entity. But if the I-thought were suddenly to cease to exist, the "worthless loser" concept-clothing would have nothing to hang on and would collapse in a heap —and along with it the whole illusory personal scarecrow-self. Note that this same principle applies to "dual reactions" as well: I am afraid, I am angry, I am offended, I am jealous, etc. Remove the I-thought, and the fear, anger, offense, jealousy, etc., would have nothing that could sustain their existence, for all of these depend on an "I" that feels them and "becomes" them.

Now this fact of "I-thought-as-host" obviously suggests a different liberation technique from the one we developed in the previous sections. There, our emphasis was on dismantling the hanger-on concepts—clearly an important and desirable goal. But with that approach, no matter how many concepts (or reactions) we succeed in removing, the I-thought will still remain to host others—and will continue to do so endlessly. Thus we need a meditation designed to weaken and eventually remove the I-thought itself. If we could do this, it would represent the ultimate solution to our concept and reaction problems, since no counterfeit "I" would remain who could be a worthless loser, or offended, or anything else. Further, it would free us—at least partially—of the necessity of laboriously dismantling, one by one, each individual concept or lower-nature reaction.

Now many readers might be skeptical whether anyone but a meditator of many years' experience could have any realistic chance of succeeding at such a seemingly audacious undertaking. But in my experience of both using the PLS and teaching it to a variety of people (including meditation novices), attacking the I-thought has never failed to produce beneficial effects for anyone willing to try. Here is a meditation to experiment with.

PLS Meditation for Weakening & Removing the I-Thought

- Note the presence of the I-thought and the false self at its core.
- Note the facade/mask/persona that is built up around it.
- Note how tiring and tiresome it is to support these artificial entities.
  - Recall the times you've felt, "I'm so tired of myself."
  - Note that what was tiring was not your real identity, but your artificial one & all its reactions, limitations, desires, needs, etc.
- Now direct your attention inward.
  - Let it "float" backwards into the region of your head center.
  - Look "upward" and feel for the Self and its world of reality.
- Now Self-aligned and "I-thought-aware," activate your imagination.
  - Imagine, "There is no [*fill in your name here*]."
  - Note all the not-self concepts associated with this I-thought-name: age, sex, appearance, memories, relationships, obligations, etc.
  - Feel how if [*your name + concepts*] disappeared, YOU would still exist.
  - Your real identity and individuality would be intact and unchanged.
  - Imagine at length: Who would I be without this I-thought?
  - Feel how foreign/artificial the I-thought is compared with the Self.
  - Feel what a burden the I-thought is & what a relief it is to shed it.
- Experiment with applying the same imagination to other people.
  - Imagine, "There is no [*fill in another person's name here*]."
  - Note all the not-self concepts associated with this I-thought-name.
  - Note that his/her I-thought creates a false self as unreal as yours.
  - Note that his/her real Self is as grand & unlimited as yours.
  - Note the effect this has on both you & your view of him/her.

AFTERWORD

In contemplating how to make the Personal Liberation System available to a wider audience, I decided that a theory-and-practice approach would serve readers the best. The theory part was to write this formal "how-to" instruction manual explaining the PLS principles and techniques, and suggesting experiments for applying them. Because I wanted this manual to be short and concise, I refrained from overloading the text with extensive examples of the system at work in the lives of people using it. Instead, I opted for short examples of the artificial kind, typically "suppose that..." followed by an invented scenario. While I trust such examples were helpful and instructive, they lack the power of longer case studies from real life to demonstrate the system in actual operation and covey the full picture of its transformative potential.

To provide such case studies and thus fulfill the practice half of my task, I am presently working on a second PLS volume tentatively titled *The Personal Liberation System in Action: Dialogues With Users*. It will consist of excerpts from transcriptions of consultations I have with PLS users who solicit my advice about how best to apply the system's techniques and methods to their particular circumstances and problems. The informal (and fun) nature of these consultations, the wide variety of people and situations involved, the many experiments that I devise for them and they report about, my answers to their questions about various aspects of the system—all these combine to significantly expand the explanation of the PLS found in the present volume. These transcriptions will provide every serious PLS user with valuable practical ideas to apply to his or her own life, courtesy of kindred spirits wrestling with similar problems and using the same tools to attack and solve them.

For further information about this coming volume, as well as information about private consultations and access to supplementary materials for PLS users, please visit www.thepls.org.

BIBLIOGRAPHY

Alcyone (attributed to J. Krishnamurti). *At the Feet of the Master* (PDF–110 KB). Accessed September 20, 2015. http://www.theosophical.ca/otherdocuments/AtTheFeetOfTheMaster_AlcyoneJKrishnamurti.pdf

Aum. New York: Agni Yoga Society, Inc., 1980.

Baba Hari Dass. *Talks: Knowledge and Dispassion*. Accessed September 20, 2015. www.mountmadonna.org/yoga/talks/twb9610.html. Sri Ram Foundation, www.sriramfoundation.org.

Barker, Trevor, ed. *The Mahatma Letters to A.P. Sinnett*. Pasadena, California: Theosophical University Press, 1975

Brotherhood. New York: Agni Yoga Society, Inc., 1982.

Jinarajadasa, C., ed. *Letters From the Masters of Wisdom, Second Series*. Adyar, Madras, India: The Theosophical Publishing House, 1977.

Maharshi's Gospel, Books I & II: Being Answers of Bhagavan Sri Ramana Maharshi to Questions put to Him by Devotees. Tiruvannamalai, South India: V.S. Ramanan, President, Board of Trustees of Sri Ramanasramam, 2002.

Powell, A. E. *The Mental Body* (PDF–1486 KB). Accessed July 2, 2015. http://www.hermetics.org/pdf/theosophy/Arthur_E_Powell_-_The_Mental_Body.pdf

Who Am I? (Nan Yar?): The Teachings of Bhagavan Sri Ramana Maharshi. Translated from the original Tiruvannamalai, South India: V.S. Ramanan, President, Board of Trustees of Sri Ramanasramam.

www.ingramcontent.com/pod-product-compliance
Lightning Source LLC
Chambersburg PA
CBHW060529100426
42743CB00009B/1465